"Unlike other books available on the subject of loss, here is a front-row seat to the process of grieving. Through a compilation of writings written through the first year of loss, Dr. Perry Hubbard has given us a rare glimpse of the raw emotions, thoughts, struggles, complications, and messiness that is grief. Through his journey, and willingness to be vulnerable, we can gain hope, insight, grace for ourselves and for others who are struggling through the process as well. Perry cuts through the platitudes and tells it like it is, addressing difficult issues like fairness and anger, and shares his own personal journey through poems and reflections written as he experienced the process firsthand."

**Rev. Rod Zottarelli,** MA,
Wellness Coach – Global Partners

---

"Grieving the loss of his wife and ministry partner, Perry expresses thoughts and feelings on grief from a deeply personal perspective. With each chapter, there is a growing desire to know and to identify with him as his thoughts on grief touch the very heart and soul of the reader."

**Tim Mills,** Psy.D., Clinical Psychologist,
Private Practice, New Direction Counseling, Holland, MI

---

# My Book of Grief: A Man's Perspective

# My Book of Grief:

## *A Man's Perspective*

Dr. Perry J. Hubbard

Sea Hill Press Inc.
www.seahillpress.com

ISBN: 9798642268155

Printed in the United States of America.

# Dedication

This book is dedicated to my wife Nancy R Hubbard.
We were together for almost forty years. We knew from almost the first
day we met each other that we were meant for each other.

Thank you for all those years of love,
Your loving husband

# Contents

# Introduction

I have not really dealt with grief at a personal and profound level until the death of my wife. As a result, I have not always been as sympathetic as one probably should be when others are grieving. I just didn't understand what was happening.

When my wife died, I began to understand grief. I say "began" because I have come to realize that grief has many forms, many levels, and many ways of being expressed. There is the simple grief that occurs when we see death portrayed in the media. There is the grief that happens when life is snuffed out by accident or disease. When these occur, we feel a sense of loss.

There is a deeper type of grief when relatives, close friends, and co-workers die. There is the more profound grief that occurs when a parent, a sibling, or a close family member dies. Then there is the incredibly complicated and intense grief that occurs when a spouse of many years dies. When these occur, our life is altered.

This book is about the latter.

Some have recommended books to read, scriptures to read, and sent images and poems with the intent of helping me as I dealt with my grief. I consciously chose not to make use of them. I wanted to let my grief teach me first and then compare what I had learned with others.

As I processed my grief, I found a couple of people who were willing to read what I was writing. This was important because if one is not careful one can be so absorbed in what is happening, they become trapped. Trapped in a stage or aspect of grief and unable to move forward. Their comments helped to assure me that I was doing reasonably well in processing my grief. They also helped me to keep moving forward and remain open to what would come next.

This book represents my journey. It involves three types of materials.

My insights into various aspects of grief, poems about grief, and finally reflections on how my grief impacted my life, emotions, and thoughts.

I will be honest, this is a man's perspective. And I will be even more honest, as I wrote I chose not to fight the tears and emotions. For some, that means I wasn't very manly, but for me it allowed me to become more of a man, a fully mature man, one not afraid of his emotions and willing to face them and share them with others.

One more thing: You will not find a lot of scripture references in this material. But if you pay attention you will see the influence of my relationship with God and the presence of his truth throughout. Truthfully, one cannot fully deal with death in a mature human manner if they don't have a deep and sincere knowledge of the truth and its author.

I hope that what I have written will be helpful and useful to those in the midst of their grief. Not everyone can find the words to express what is happening. I also hope that it will do the same for those trying to understand and comfort those dealing with grief.

Perry J. Hubbard

# The Beginning

I have included three things from the beginning of our life together. The first is the prayer we wrote and put in the program for our wedding. The second is my grandmother's prayer for us as we began our marriage. The last is our vows. We wrote them; it was in style to do this back then. I share them to give a sense of where things started and a point of reference, an idea of the foundation that our marriage was built on and so influenced the form of my grief.

## Our Wedding Prayer

> Lord, to You we give our thanks
>      For Your presence in this
>                     Celebration
> Lord, without You there is no life
>      No possibility of celebration.
> Lord, again then, we thank You
>      And hope that in this event
>                Your name will be praised

## Prayer of Olive Hubbard, Perry's grandmother, written for the wedding

We present to Thee, for thy loving and wise care and guidance, Perry and Nancy, who are entering a life of togetherness.

May the happiness they feel today be only a token of what the years will bring.

We ask that Thou wilt give enough hurts to make them humbly sympathetic and helpful witnesses, and enough victories to always look back, to face confidence and courage.

May they always feel the responsibility their talents and heritage entail. Keep their hands in Thine, and each other's.

So should the years be happy and fruitful, and they shall be contented in any circumstance.

And so shall The kingdom come and They will be done in the lives and hearts of Mr. and Mrs. Perry Hubbard. Amen.

# Wedding Vows

Together:
Nancy – Perry
    I love you.
    And I have waited all of my life to be able to say
            These three words to you.
And on this day, I have also decided to say them before
            These people.


Perry:
Nancy – I love you.
    And I hope to share this love with you
            From this day until the Lord calls
                Either of us home.


Nancy:
Perry – I love you.
    And today I pledge you my love
            From this day forward.


Perry:
Nancy – I love you.
    And I realize that this means I am including you
                In my life
                        To make it our life
                Whatever it will be
                        Wherever it will be
                In the Lord's will.


Nancy:
Perry – I love you.
    And wherever we are,
            In whatever circumstance we might be in.
    I'll be by your side.

Perry:
Nancy – I love you.
    In these words, I commit to your care all of my being.
        My time, and most important,
            Me.
        My thoughts, my feelings; that which is most truly me,
            And which is most fragile.

Nancy:
Perry – I love you.
    And, everything that I have, and every part of me,
Now becomes part of you.
I give you my time,
My deepest thoughts and feelings
My emotions, and most of all – my love

Perry:
Nancy – I love you.
    I accept you into my life;
        To care for you, to be near you.
    No matter what I feel like.
    To be for you all that you need me to be.

Nancy:
Perry – I love you.
    I'll be at your side to meet your needs,
        Your wants and desires.
    To be all that you want and need me to be.

Together:
Nancy – Perry
    I love you
    I thank the Lord for you and
        Desire that we together –
    Will on this day – our wedding day –
    Give our life together over to God for His use and honor.
    I love you
        And today, I thee wed.

Thoughts on Different Aspects of Grief

# I Want to Be Angry, but Why?

I want to be angry. I think I should be angry. It is my right to be angry. Isn't it?

I mean it is one of the steps of grief. At some point, I am supposed to be angry. I have suffered a loss, not just any loss, but a loss that creates such pain and sorrow. I have a right to be angry about this. It is not fair. It is not right.

She should not have died now and caused me such pain. Okay, it wasn't her fault, but it sure feels like she is somehow to blame for my pain. If she had not done this or had listened and followed the ideas and suggestions of others. If she had just paid attention and not let this happen.

I was not ready for this to happen. God, why did you let this happen?

And then there are the people who say such stupid things to me. They say something that only reveals they have no idea of what I am experiencing. They share scriptures, poems, and platitudes that only reveal how little they understand. They send a note they think will be helpful but only reminds me of my pain. Oh, and the ones who send a note to all those suffering a loss. How impersonal is that? Like assuming everyone is the same and that one good note will be helpful to everyone. So impersonal. It makes me want to be angry.

I want to be angry. I think I should be angry. I have a right to be angry. Just leave me alone and let me be angry.

But why should I be angry?

First, let us make the context clear. There are many things that can cause a person to be angry. The focus here is on the anger that can come because of grief and loss. The anger that is caused by something we have no control over and cannot change. So, let's think about anger and what may be happening as we deal with anger.

Let us begin by considering why we are dealing with anger.

**I have a right to be angry.**

Is it really my right?

Do any of us have a right to be angry at what happens in life? It doesn't matter what you believe, we are all taught from a very early age that one day we will die. If your belief leaves you with little hope for what will happen after you die then to die early, unexpectedly, or without reason can make a person angry. Angry because of the feeling that something was stolen, taken prematurely, and they didn't get to have what everyone else might enjoy when they live longer.

If you are a person with a faith and belief that there is something more beyond death, then what is the reason for your anger? You should be excited about what lies ahead, unless you believe that there may be severe punishment waiting for you. Then anger may come because there was not enough time for the person to get things right and be able to avoid the dangerous in order to experience the pleasure or good of what comes next. Yes, that might cause you to be angry.

But if they are a Christian and were forgiven, they will join others in heaven with God. Then what does death mean? It is a transition that allows a person to depart the struggle of this world to enjoy all that God has promised. So, why are you angry that someone has been allowed to leave the struggle of this world to enter heaven and enjoy all that has been promised?

So, do I have a right to be angry? Or, more importantly, do I have the right to celebrate?

**It is necessary to be angry.**

Psychologists suggest that anger is a natural part of the grieving process. You will be angry about the loss and angry at any number of things and people. The doctors, other family members, friends, and on the list can go. There may be a need to be angry at yourself because you somehow failed to do what needed to be done to prevent the death of your loved one.

You may be angry because you didn't do any number of things you, and others, feel you should have done. You know, said I love you more, hugged the person more, called the person more often, and on this list can go. An especially difficult one is where I am angry because I didn't say I was sorry, didn't mend the rift in the relationship, or didn't do what was expected of me in the past.

In some of these, anger is a real concern. You should be angry about your failures. You will need to face them and deal with what you did or didn't do. The danger is in taking your anger out on others and in a way blaming them and punishing them for your failure.

The most difficult anger to deal with is when someone else did what is wrong, failed in some way, or worse, in some way was the cause of the death of your loved one. The issue now is not the death of the loved one, but a feeling of being robbed and wanting to make that person pay. But can anyone really pay and in making the payment give you back what you lost?

Is anger necessary? Or does it merely get in the way of truly dealing with the loss and the issues that need to be cared for? Anger will not return the person, anger will not fix what happened, and anger will never be able to force a payment sufficient to restore what was lost.

This is not a broken toy that can be repaired or replaced. It is not a car that you can send to a body shop for them to restore it to its original condition. It is not a broken bone that, with proper care, will mend itself.

No, it is final, and nothing can change what has happened.

Am I being a little cold? Maybe. But I am being honest.

As a Christian, I know that I live in a sinful world and death is an expected outcome for every life. I can choose to be angry or I can choose to not be angry and be able to help myself and others deal with the grief and loss. In every situation and context: When it is the death after a long and fruitful life. When it is death that comes suddenly from disaster and accidents. When it is death caused by sickness and disease. And yes, like a friend of mine whose daughter was killed by an inattentive driver, even learn to love and care for those who have caused the death of my loved one.

The problem is not what happens but a lack of preparedness for death. We don't treat life as a blessing from God, so when death comes, we are angry because, to be honest, we didn't know how to live and help others to live.

**I failed.**

I am angry because I should have done something, and if I had done it, they would be alive or not suffering as much. I am angry because in some way I failed to show my love and concern. I failed to say, "I am sorry," or to say, "I forgive you." I am angry because I was selfish and didn't take care of business and them, until it was too late. I am angry because you died, and I wasn't ready.

There are several layers to this type of anger. The first is the anger that comes because of something we didn't do and now the opportunity to act has been lost. As a result you don't know what to do with that frustration and feeling of guilt, so you become angry. The anger is mainly directed at yourself but can easily spill over to those around you. They want to soothe your pain, they want to calm your anger, they want to forgive you, but you won't allow it because they cannot speak for the person that has died. Or you won't let them.

If this is the source of your anger, then until you allow someone else to speak words of comfort and forgiveness you will remain angry. Until you realize that you will never be able to correct your failure concerning that specific person and situation, you will remain angry. Until you learn a key lesson, to forgive yourself, you will remain angry. Until you learn to forgive yourself and use what you have learned to improve how you treat others and help others, you will remain angry.

If we are to be honest, there is a long list of things we should have done but will never get to do. Or it's reverse, things we shouldn't have done, which can never be undone. Until we accept our responsibility, allow ourselves to be forgiven and forgive ourselves, we cannot make the changes needed to bring an end to this type of anger.

**It is unfair and that makes me angry.**

That is a common reason people use for their anger. It isn't fair. It is not right. They didn't deserve to die, or it wasn't the right time to die. And so on.

We confuse the meaning of this word "fair." We think in terms of being on a level playing field and everything being run smoothly and efficiently. We think everyone has the same rights and opportunities. And so, when it doesn't go as we expect or think it should, it is somehow unfair. As if we had the right to have what we want.

Take a short pause to consider what is happening in the world. That should serve to create a lot of questions with this type of thinking. If "fair" is the correct word to use, then there is a lot of unfairness in the world. Is it fair for a baby to be born in the jungle and exposed to so much disease that it has a one in five chance of living to the age of two? Is it fair that people are subjected to the rule of tyrants? Is it fair that because of the state of a location many will die of hunger? Is it fair . . . ?

To be honest, you will never be able to answer those questions. And death never seems fair, no matter where you live and what is happening. Especially the death of a child or death from an accident, or death from cancer that takes a person before their time, or at least what we think is their time.

And to be more honest, the word "fair" is a trap. "Fair" means everyone gets the same result, same blessing, same opportunity, same trouble, and that is not possible. We may have been created that way, to have an equal measure of all that God wanted for us, but we messed that up. The fact that we are alive and can know God is more than any of us deserves.

Until we deal with the reality, we will believe everything is unfair and seek something to blame, seek someone to blame, even God.

**I have been hurt and it makes me angry.**

It is true, the loss of a loved one causes much pain and hurt. Loss in any of its forms makes us hurt. Loss of trust, physical loss from injury or sickness, loss of friendship, and loss to death. They all create pain, physical and emotional pain. And we need to be clear, emotional loss does cause a physical effect.

The pain from injury and sickness can sometimes be dealt with. There are medical resources to help with that. For the more severe events, while medicine cannot provide for restoration, it can provide means to manage what has happened. There are treatments for things like diabetes, artificial help like prosthetics, and special equipment for the more severely handicapped. In these, the level of hurt will depend on the person, their capacity to manage the loss, and the support group they may have.

But with the loss of a loved one through death, there is no medicine, no prosthetics, or special equipment. You cannot replace what has been lost. You can't find another person to fill that space.

So, you are hurt, feel helpless, and you are angry.

And you want an answer and explanation for why it happened at this time and in this way. Unfortunately, there is no answer. We cannot explain why someone dies when they do or in the way they do. We cannot say why a good person – one loved by all – dies, when another person – who is in our eyes evil – lives a long and healthy life.

This was a point of contention between Job and his friends. Job was correct in stating it is not about how good or bad a person is. But though he was right in this aspect, he could not explain why, any more than his friends could. Their idea of the wicked suffering and dying young failed when faced with all that happened to Job.

So, I hurt, and it can't be explained why this happened at this time, and so I am angry.

    But angry at what? Or who?

    And that will be our next area to consider.

    Who am I angry at?

# Who Am I Angry At?

Let's start by making a list of those we might be angry at:

- Others – that indistinct group of people who we target because we have no other target.
- Offender 1 – this is the word for all those who may have directly caused the death of a person. The driver in a car, the thief, a soldier, and others. They may have made a mistake, acted as required by others, or acted in a selfish way.
- Offender 2 – sometimes people cause the death of someone unintentionally. It differs from the driver in the car. They mismanaged their rights and caused someone's death.
- Medical – this is the group of people that had the responsibility to solve any and all problems of the health and recovery of a person.
- Friends – anyone close to me that I can blame for anything.
- Family – my family, the other person's family, any family member.
- Religious leaders – the pastors, healers, and others.
- Fate – an uncontrollable force that makes us angry.
- God – he has ultimate control and we are angry with his action and decision.

And now an attempt to understand why we would be angry with them.

## *Others*

There are times when we feel the actions and attitudes of others contributed to the cause of our loss. At times we can identify a group or pattern followed by people that contributed to and even caused the event: a company that polluted a water source and so caused cancer in many people; a tradition or custom that creates dangerous situations; a protest gone bad. There are many events and activities in this world that can and often do result in serious injury and death to those we call the innocent.

Should we be angry at them? Probably, especially if they knew what the possible results would be and chose to ignore that and proceed with their activity. This anger can take one of two actions: It can go out of control and seek to damage anyone associated with what has happened, or it can become focused and act to correct the situation before it affects others.

It is unfortunate that too often this anger moves in the direction of revenge and payback. They took someone from me, and so they need to pay. But the payment desired is often excessive, sufficient to ruin them, and in the end, causes more innocent people to suffer as well. This level of anger often cannot differentiate between those actually responsible and those who are pawns in the process. The janitor of the building may have no idea what the boss is doing and yet is attacked because of association.

If the anger is properly focused, it can be used to bring about change, sometimes. It is unfortunate that too often those most responsible are also those least likely to respond to an adult handling of anger. Too often, if there is no threat to their way of life or safety, they ignore this until sufficient pressure is brought to bear.

If there is no response, then the anger may be refocused on others – friends and family – because of the frustration and lack of a proper outlet to the anger.

## *Offender 1*

We are angry with those who intentionally cause the death of our loved one: The thief who shoots someone during a robbery, the rapist who kills their victim, the drunken driver who knows they should not be driving and yet does so, and in the end, cause an accident and the death of others. We could expand this to dictators, criminal bosses, gang members, and others who intentionally plan and carry out the death of others. Sadly, innocent people are often caught in the crossfire and die, and that brings on our anger.

As above with the others, there is a right to be angry. And as above, there are two responses, revenge or seeking a manner to rectify the situation.

Actually, there is a third option that should be presented. Even if you do all you can to fix a situation, it will not bring back the person who is now dead. At some point, we will have to consider if we need to learn to forgive the offender. If not, the anger will simply grow like a cancer in us until it begins to affect others, even those near us.

We have many examples of this being done in Scriptures. Two key ones are Jesus forgiving those crucifying him, and Stephen forgiving those stoning him. A key teaching of Jesus was to forgive your enemies. To be honest, uncontrolled anger is a greater enemy and destroyer than the one who caused the death of our loved one. It will consume you and another life will be destroyed.

## *Offender 2*

We need this category because there are what we call accidents. Actions that are unintentional but cause death. A key example is that of a child running out into traffic and being hit by a car.

The anger is directed at the person who caused the death when it really wasn't their fault. It's the wrong-place, wrong-time concept. But we are angry because we want to blame someone and even ourselves. It is almost a knee-jerk type of reaction. The shock creates a need to respond, to release the sudden explosion of emotion and the person lashes out. The most likely target, the one who caused the event. The next potential target, surprisingly, can be the person who has just died. As if unleashing my anger on them will somehow help.

This is a dangerous release of anger. If not dealt with correctly, it becomes a poison in the system of the griever and slowly will destroy all the good that existed between them, their memories, shared life, and future hopes. It was their fault, and now their actions are causing me to suffer.

This is a very difficult type of anger to defuse since the person who caused it is dead and cannot respond and say I am sorry or provide any other words of comfort. Nor can anyone else do that for them.

## *Medical personnel*

This is anyone who is involved in the medical care and treatment of my loved one that becomes a target of my anger. The focus is either on the belief that they did not do enough or the right thing, or what they did didn't help and even may have accelerated the process.

This anger is based on a feeling of helplessness. Something we feel as we watch a person who is sick or injured die, and there is nothing that seems to make a difference in stopping the process or even slowing the process. In this helplessness, our hope is placed in these professionals who we consider capable of fixing and healing anything, will do what we want, and prevent death.

We don't want to hear the words, "There is nothing more we can do," or, "We have tried everything possible," or, "The cancer has progressed too far," or "The damage was just too severe." We have heard too many stories of people recovering from incredibly severe injuries and advanced stages of sickness. The Internet feeds us this information with offers of miracle plans, drugs, foods, and practices that will restore life. As a result, we expect the same thing to happen for us.

The anger is really about the truth that we cannot control death. Even when we know it is imminent, it is an inexorable foe and will, short of a miracle, bring life to an end. Still, we hold on to the belief that this group can do something. There has to be another medicine, treatment, or procedure that will stop our loved one from dying.

While malpractice may be a legitimate reason for anger, there is, in the background, the reality of the fragile nature of life. There would not have been the possibility of malpractice if there were no problems with our bodies. In this case, the issue is more about dying too soon, before their time, because of the negligence or poor choices and actions of one committed to not harming but helping.

Properly used, the anger can bring an end to poor practice but will not have any effect on recovering what has been lost. And clearly, we need to avoid attaching blame to those who have done their best to restore life, or at least maintain it, until we have had time to process what is happening.

And that is the key issue, time to process.

From here on the who becomes more difficult.

## Friends

It is amazing how often friends become the brunt or target of anger. The person becomes angry with them for any number of reasons:

- They are intruding in my world, and I don't want them around.
- They don't understand what I am going through and should stop trying to help.
- Their words are insensitive and useless.
- They should have been here when I needed them.
- They should be doing something, they could have done something, they are doing this and not that or that and not this.

There are probably many more. This anger is, in many ways, not really directed at the friends. It is about the feeling of helplessness and frustration that wells up within and anyone handy becomes the target of a release of anger.

I will admit that a friend who uses too many platitudes and is insensitive could rightfully cause the anger of which they become the target. It makes sense. Too often people will say anything without considering what they are saying, and that lack of sensitivity triggers the anger. Even saying that something helped someone else with their loss can trigger this anger. It is because we are not talking about someone else, and to be lumped together with everyone else is offensive. I am not everyone else.

And this is what causes us to be angry with people we call friends and acquaintances.

## Family

While in many ways this is very similar to what can happen to friends, it will be different. One of the key reasons is when there is a rift in our relationship with our family, we see that as a failure on their part to be what we think they need to be and do for us. It rarely matters that they are not a factor in the death; they just aren't close enough emotionally as we think they should be.

Family relations can be so complicated. Small things, forgotten, taken lightly, or misconstrued become lightning rods that cause anger to well up and strike.

They are easy targets because they are close. So, if a person is not alert, this can cause a backlash and the anger will flow in reverse. Them to you, because if they are not sensitive to the issues of loss through death, they will take your anger personally and respond in like manner. This can become especially serious if they think you have failed in a way in which they perceive compounded the process of death or contributed to it.

At this point, the debate could become about who has the right to be angry. My loss is greater than yours. The person was my family member, sister, brother, etc. Sometimes there could be a feeling that you took the person away from them, physically or emotionally. This opens the door for you to be angry about how they responded and them to the separation you caused.

If you don't quickly deal with this, you will all risk creating severe and deep schisms that may become almost irreparable, all because you became angry at family, rightly or wrongly.

## Religious leaders

Unfortunately, many place an unreasonable level of responsibility on these people, much like the medical personnel. The difference here is, it is anger about what they didn't do, didn't have the faith to do, or in acting as we expected and hoped they should do, we felt faith was too weak to produce results.

We call on these people when we need miracles, or at least when we think we need more done than what any human being can do through medicine, treatment, and protection. We believe they are supposed to have unique access to spiritual power to bring about these miracles.

When we don't get the desired results, we become angry at them. Most religious structures encourage their followers to go to key people to pray, to learn what rituals to perform, and what sacrifices or changes need to be made in order to get the healing desired.

When they try to explain why nothing worked, the explanations only cause frustration and anger. It is not in God's plan, you did it all wrong, or you didn't believe in what you were doing are a few of those explanations.

As a result, we become angry because we feel like we have been deceived in some way, that we have been given false hope only to have everything crumble around us. Dealing with the death of someone is difficult enough, but to have your hopes raised up only to have everything crash around you can cause a profound loss of trust and a seething anger toward those who promote and proclaim such hope.

A lot of how a person reacts will depend greatly on the depth of their relationship with their faith and what it teaches about life, death, and what happens afterward. For some, there is great hope even in death, and a failure to receive healing is seen in the light of a greater good. For some, there is very little hope and a failure to receive the desired result can plunge them into deep despair, which can spark anger at those who, in their minds, promised much but delivered little.

It is because we believe these people are supposed to have some special connection and insight into obtaining miracles and answers. When they fail, we can lose more than the person, we can lose our anchors and direction as well. We can lose our ability to function and the confidence that everything has a purpose.

### Fate

I wasn't sure if this should be before or after religious leaders. In some structures, they are entwined until they are almost inseparable. If fate has decreed death, then nothing can change that. The only reason that a miracle would come is that fate has decreed it.

The most common, but certainly not the only things that cause this kind of thinking, are disasters. Disasters make no sense. The sudden loss of so much life and the destruction of so many things is hard to grasp for the one trapped in the moment.

But such events are not caused only by earthquakes, tornadoes, hurricanes, and other similar events. A deer runs into a car, a sudden gust of wind brings down a tree, a branch falls and brings death. In these situations, there are no human players, no disease, just random events that catch the unwary off guard and yield the phrase, *in the wrong place at the wrong time*.

For some, there is a feeling of relief: I was just there; I was on my way but got delayed; I had just left. And we thank our lucky stars, shamrock, root, or whatever we believe might have protected us. We were fated to live. But those who were not so fortunate died, and now those who survived are left in turmoil trying to understand why.

There is a great deal of anger at the unfairness of it all. Why this one and not another? Why now and not later? The problem is how do you get angry at a wind, a wave, or an object that has no mind of its own and did not have any part in deciding when they would blow, move, or fall. Yet the anger is real. And it hunts for a target to release its energy.

Maybe not at first, but in time, it will lash out and try to blame someone for failing to do something. If not anger, an incredibly debilitating type of desolation can set in. There is no hope, life makes no sense, and living is futile. In this level of desolation, there is anger within it, and it will attack anyone who tries to tell them otherwise, tries to help them to live again, and suggests that hope can be restored.

There is not enough time to go into all that happens when fate is the object of one's anger, and I know clearly that I do not have enough understanding of how it affects those living in its shadow to say more than I have.

## God

God is always a possible target for our anger. He created the world, he supposedly made everything good, and yet there is so much evil. Over and over people have asked why bad things happen to good people. Why God does not heal those who truly believe? Why God does not answer all of our prayers?

Anger that is focused on God is based on faulty information and understanding. Yes, he created everything, and it was supposed to be good. The problem is that we do not behave in a manner that will allow that good to exist. And in many ways, our existence, as individuals, would not be possible if it weren't for God. We do not get what we deserve for our sins.

But don't tell that to someone who has just lost a loved one. To them,

God is the problem. He created us and should do everything possible to keep us healthy and safe; and when he doesn't, we blame him and release our anger at him.

The image is one of two things: God is all-powerful and doesn't really care what happens. God is all-powerful and cares but has chosen not to do what we want or desire. Either way, God is at fault and we are angry. We just don't see how letting our loved one die could be an expression of love. This is especially true of the death of a baby or child. We think they had so much to live for and are angry that he chose to let the life end and steal from us all that we desired in that relationship.

We will remain angry, like Job's wife, at God and blame him for what has happened when in fact he did not cause the events that resulted in the death of workers and family. He simply did not intervene in the way she desired. Job saw this and asked if we should only accept from God the good and not the bad as well. A partially correct idea because more often than not the cause is not God. Good and bad are part of life. What God brings is a new view of what life is. It is a state where you can experience him no matter what may be happening at any given moment. What he gives is a unique good, him.

When we see that reality, then what is happening – the loss, the pain – can open new doors and access to him and the real good that he has always promised to give in any setting and situation.

Sometimes learning this is easy and other times it is very difficult. The death of a loved one in old age who has walked with God all their life is easier to deal with and is often seen as a blessing. The opposite is the death of a child who had a whole life ahead of them.

In between are so many others: Life-threatening illnesses and injuries that bring death unexpectedly, before we think it should come. The death of one who has known the truth but refuses to listen. In each, we can become angry at God for not intervening and giving more time to us and them.

That brings us to the last object of our anger. It was touched on briefly in the first area of *why*. It will be worth reviewing this in greater depth

# Who? — Angry at Me?

Yes, we can and do get angry at ourselves over the death of a loved one. The cause of this anger is usually any regrets or guilt we have concerning the person. These regrets and guilt occur at several levels with varying degrees of impact and potentially serious consequences. Let me list what I think are the different causes:

- I am directly involved in causing the death of the person. My actions put them in harm's way. (These are things like a bad decision or inattentiveness while driving.) I did something that caused a sequence of events that puts the person in harm's way. (This could be the careless handling of a firearm and many others.)
- I am indirectly involved in the cause of the death of the person. My inattention to them or mistreatment resulted in them acting in a way that resulted in their death. (Some suicides could be placed in this category.) I feel that I did something that pushed them over the edge.
- I am indirectly involved because I was not paying attention and was not able to do something that could have saved the person.

These three listed above are very serious forms of regret that create profound levels of guilt. These three are beyond the scope of what I want to consider here.

- I regret saying or doing something that hurt the person, and I failed to resolve the issue before they died. I judged them unfairly, criticized them publicly, opposed them unreasonably and so on.
- I regret not saying or doing something that I should have done; like not honoring them, showing them respect, appreciating their skills and abilities, encouraging them, and so on.
- I regret the little things that I did that annoyed and frustrated the person because I was insensitive.
- I regret not paying more attention to them when I should have, because I was selfish.
- I regret not sharing more of my time, thoughts, feelings, and on this list goes.

- I regret not having told them I love them or hugged them one more time. I should have listened more (and on this list goes as well).
- I regret not doing what they wanted to do, at some recent point in time.

As you can see there are basically two forms of regret on this list: What I didn't do and what I did do. The what I didn't do list will be a challenge because you cannot ever do anything to correct that completely. You may be able to confess those issues to others, family and friends, but it will always be lacking in some way. You may be able to act the way you should have now and please others with the change. This is not about your sincerity and honesty in the process. It is the fact that the person cannot hear and respond to you.

These things apply to the area of *what I did that I wish I could undo*. How do you take back harsh words, insensitive actions, criticism, and anything you did you now see as wrong? You can't, any more than you can do what you didn't do. And that creates regret.

The regret remains, and there are two options.

One is to become angry and punish yourself for your failures. You become judge, lawyer, and jury and convict yourself of the crime, and then become the executioner of whatever sentence you impose on yourself. The angrier you are the more serious your self-imposed punishment can be. The only way out of this situation will be your ability to forgive yourself. There is no amount of anger and subsequent punishment that can pay the debt you have imposed on yourself.

How you get to the point of forgiveness is a road with many options. It is like driving in a city from one point to another. There are many routes, some more direct, and others that are indirect. Direct because you deal with it and few others are involved. More indirect because you have to make other stops along the way to share and demonstrate your chagrin over your actions to others who were also affected by what you didn't do.

I need to stop here and correct an error about the two forms of regret. I said there were two sources: the "didn't do" and the "did do." While in a sense they are two areas that cause regret, in reality, they are part of the same group of actions that had a negative impact on the relationship. So, two sides of the same coin. It doesn't matter which side lands up when tossed, it still reveals a negative type of regret.

The other regret is about not doing more. Or better stated wishing I had done more of what brought us both pleasure and joy: the actions, words, and responses that bonded us together in a unique way and were the foundation on which we lived. A relational structure that gave strength to face whatever was happening, whether it was the capacity to experience all of the joy available, or the strength to deal with any challenges confronted.

I regret not doing it more, not so much because I was somehow deficient in demonstrating my love, the nature of our relationship, or understanding of each other. I regret it because of the hope that if I had done it more, the outcome would somehow have been affected and I would still be enjoying those hugs, those quiet moments, those shared thoughts and emotions, and so much more.

The regret exists because I no longer have access to all of that and I yearn for them. I want to hug, kiss, cuddle, talk, be silent one more time, so that somehow, I might still experience it now. And I struggle with this because, as real as the memory is, I cannot feel what I cry out for. And I regret that I did not do more of something so that I would not feel so empty now and not able to enjoy the memory of all that we had.

If I follow that path, then anger can set in again. I may blame myself, I may even blame the one I lost, because of this regret. It is my fault, and so I become angry for not doing enough to somehow change what I feel now.

Like all before, it is not possible to go back. You cannot get one more hug. You can only imagine it because it is imprinted in your being. You can almost feel it, but when your eyes open, it is your pillow or some other object. And then the regret and the loss hit and spin you around.

I had better stop here. It is not wise to regret doing the right thing more. It can lead to confusion in our relations with others if we try to use them as replacements, as stunt doubles. They suffer the action but receive none of the rewards because it was not for them, it was for someone else. You get one more hug, but you are not thinking about the person giving you the hug but the one you lost, and you both lose in the process. They are not being treated properly, and you are only deceiving yourself.

Regrets about a conversation you didn't have. Regrets about not discussing a sensitive issue. Regrets about not doing and saying more. As you can see it is not hard to expand the list of regrets.

If one is not careful, the regrets can create guilt. A desire to place the blame on me. And when there is blame, the door is opened to anger for what has been done or not done or not sufficiently done. From there, we are back at becoming judge, jury, and executioner.

Stop for a moment and listen to my next thought: Regrets are not bad, wrong, or something to be feared. Only when they are mismanaged and allowed to take control are they a problem. When managed correctly, they can help us understand the great gift we have received, and in learning this, be able to share it with others. When managed correctly, they help us correct crucial areas in ourselves so we can be better individuals. When managed correctly, they help us do what we need to do and undo what needs to be undone.

This process may bring us to a point of anger. And at times it is correct to be angry with our behavior and actions. But only if the regret and associated guilt and anger give us the ability to make the changes that are needed. My regrets can become the foundation for living at a new level and in a new way, and of benefiting others.

# Grief — The Question

There is a question that we ask each other every day. In fact, it is almost a universal action, no matter what culture you are part of. You ask people, "How are you?" It is a formality and part of greeting friends, family, and almost everyone else that you have or want to have a reasonable relation with.

The answer is, in general, "I am okay." It doesn't matter if it is or isn't the truth, that is the standard response expected to the question. We don't really want to know more; we are just being polite and following the standard protocols of asking "the question" as part of greeting another person. And they know that they are not expected to share any details about why they are okay or not okay.

That is the level of interaction and expectation of people in most settings. And, in general, that is all that is required of both participants. Neither side wants to know more or share more, and if there is the expectation of more information, the person asking it will make the other person a bit uncomfortable and uncertain about what to share and what may be expected. If for some reason the person being asked "the question" begins to respond with information about anything beyond the standard response, then the asker becomes uncomfortable because they don't know why they are receiving such additional information nor what to do with what is being shared.

This is what happens at the basic level of interaction. This all changes if there is more than a casual relationship or encounter involved or something other than a public greeting setting.

Here is an idea of different levels where there is an expectation of more information.

- The two people involved are good friends and want to know more and are expected to share more.
- The two people involved are in a professional relation, doctor or counselor and there is an expectation of receiving more information.
- The two people have experienced an event where both have been affected and are seeking help from each other in processing what has happened.

In these situations, the question carries the expectation of more information and no one is stressed or confused by receiving more detail.

There is a third setting, and this one can become emotionally challenging. This is when one person has experienced a traumatic event in their life: an accident, a serious illness, or loss of someone close to them through death. Now when "the question" is asked, an unusual sense of uncertainty can enter.

They ask knowing that your world and life have been damaged, physically and emotionally. And you know that they have some knowledge of what has happened. The problem at this level is that neither person knows what to do next. If you say you are okay, do they dare ask more and risk being cut off? If you want to share more, you are uncertain how they will respond to the information. As a result, there is an uncomfortable pause in the conversation, and you both look for some other topic to ease the tension and move away from further discomfort.

How complicated this becomes is affected by the nature of the relationship and several factors, related to time and place, such as how often the question is being asked by that person, whether it is a frequent occurrence (several times a day), spaced out in my life (daily, weekly), or occasional (for lack of contact with the person). If they ask too often, discomfort for the one being asked can grow, and they will begin avoiding the person who appears too inquisitive, too intrusive.

Too infrequent, and there is doubt about the sincerity of their asking anything more than the standard, "How are you?" We question their right to expect more information of a personal nature.

In between are the rest. The people we see regularly. People that have always asked "the question" and to whom we have always given the standard response, I am okay. Now, though, there is an uncertainty hanging in the air. We both know what has happened, we both know that I may be struggling with any number of issues, but neither of us is quite sure what information is being sought, and what is acceptable to share.

In general, I don't want to say much. Especially as time passes. At first, I may be willing to share something about the struggle, how my schedule and activities have changed, what I miss from before that I no longer can enjoy, or something similar. Beyond that, there is no interest to discuss inner struggles, inner loss, inner frustration, and my inability to understand fully what has happened and what my future is going to look like.

To be honest, I don't believe they can begin to understand what I am experiencing, and I don't want to attempt to explain. This is because I probably have already heard many times from people that they have no idea what I am going through. They are sad but emotionally handicapped or incapable of offering any insight.

For those few who do have insight, the whole context is different. They ask "the question" and there is no need for any other comment. There is an exchange of a look, an expression of understanding that covers so much. While there are always differences in the scope of experiences involved, there is enough in common that there is an understanding of the struggle. But there will be no conversation in a public place. All of this is too private for anyone who has not been down a similar path.

That brings to mind another reason I rarely respond to those who know what has happened but have not walked a similar path. Too often their response is to quote scripture, share a story, or a song they think will be helpful. There is nothing wrong with what they share, but when you have heard this type of response over and over, you don't want to open the door again.

The problem is that some of these people decide that you *need* to hear a scripture or a word of encouragement and so share a scripture, an adage, send you cards, notes, and do so via mail, WhatsApp, email, and other means until you become insensate to them. Some of them send out their notes in a general manner. For those who may be suffering, here is a song or scripture to help you. For me, both are impersonal and represent a lack of willingness to invest the time needed to enter my world, and take the risk involved in dealing with feelings, emotions, and a life they don't understand.

It would be better for them to simply say they continue to pray and let God work. That comment is an honest confession that they know they have no words adequate to share, but they know who does and that He will respond in the best way.

And so there we stand with "the question" spoken and the standard answer given.

They wish they knew what to do – how to help, how to offer encouragement – but they don't. I wish I could speak and share the hurt, the pain, the lostness that I deal with each day, but I don't. The gulf that exists is too great. Finally, after a moment, we find another topic or simply move on to repeat the process. They are searching for those that will not create such a dilemma, and I search for the few that I may feel able to share a little, always hoping that at some point I will find someone or some manner to express what I am experiencing.

The standard question and response remain and hang in the air waiting for the right relations, right knowledge, right context so that both can move beyond it to be of help in opening the door to understanding for the one asking and freedom to share for the one being asked.

# Where Do You Live?

A friend of mine and I were chatting about some of the things I have been writing and my friend made the comment that she chose not to talk about her husband and their life together. There was a desire to share or vocalize about when her husband was alive, but over time, she had decided to be careful to not do this too much.

I recently watched a TV show that highlighted the death of a key character and how, as he interacted with a group, he constantly came back to the moment of his wife's death. The group responded and observed: That was where he was living in his thoughts and emotions. He was allowing the anger, the regret, the blame of himself and others to color all of his actions and thoughts in the present.

So, the question becomes, where do you live? How much does the past you lived with your loved one who has died color and affect your thinking? How much does it intrude into your decisions, emotions, and future life?

Not to talk at all about the life you lived before is probably unhealthy, just as to let that past have complete control of your present and future is unhealthy.

You are who you are because of your years together and all that you did together. Her presence helped form your way of thinking and living. You cannot change this. It developed your preferences and abilities and in a real way that will not fade away. Your uniqueness is intricately bound up in your past life with that person.

There is a choice to be made here before you decide how much you will share of that life and what you did together with others, as well as how you will share it. The decision is about what you talk about, the good, the bad, the common, the unusual. The choice here can have positive and negative impacts on your life.

While you may think the critical issue is about what you share, this may not be the key issue. It may be more about what you allow to dominate what you share. As in the example above, the focus was on a negative event that almost blanked out all the good that occurred before that event. While anger and blame can easily dominate what we share, the same can happen with the good history. We allow something in that past life to dominate and control our present and future. This is not good.

It is not wrong to remember. It is not wrong to share, but if that prevents you from moving forward, if that prevents you from allowing others to contribute to your life, then it will become a problem and you will live in the past. This will slowly drive people away because you have no room for them in your life. More profoundly, your actions make it clear they have nothing to contribute if it doesn't fit with your past.

The struggle is learning how not to lose the value of the past while living in the present and so create a new future. This struggle is real because of the fear of somehow losing that past, or worse finding yourself unable to remember it. Then you feel the fear that you are committing some heinous sin against the one you lost because you have not included them in the present and, in a sense, are excluding them from the future.

Now, if you want to take this to the next level, this whole process is further complicated by who you are talking to and about what you are talking.

Your immediate family – talking with your children about the one who has died – has so many facets to it. If the relationship was good, then they will want to hear the stories and be reminded. If the relationship was strained, they won't want to hear much.

If it is grandchildren, it may present a different challenge depending on their age. Too young, then they almost can't remember who you are talking about. A little older, and they will enjoy some stories but not too many. The key may be in how you share the information and stories. Tell them a good story, and they will come back for more stories. Some day they may finally ask to hear things you would like them to know but are not ready for.

Each layer of a family will have a different set of parameters and interests to consider. Is it my family asking? That will depend on how well they knew the one that has died. Is the family of the one who has died? Again, depends on many factors: how often did you get together, how did they feel about your marriage, were there any issues or concerns that may need to be dealt with? So many factors, and often they will have to be identified one by one so you can share what is appropriate and desired.

The next level is your friends. They will want to know many of the same things as the extended family. And, as in that case, the level of relationship will be critical. The more time spent together, and the quality of that time, will determine much of what they want to know and what you are willing to share.

Next, are the coworkers. This group will have a very different dynamic. The focus of what you share will shift to accommodate their knowledge of you as a couple and as individuals, their shared ministries with you as a couple and as individuals and so on.

If you are beginning to wonder if this is getting complex, you are very correct. And good for you. You are seeing that, in fact, the moment you try to keep the past alive by sharing all of it in all these formats, you are in trouble. What you share has to be appropriate to each situation, relationship, and need, and done in a way to help strengthen the now while allowing for a new future to be built without the one who has died.

Inevitably, there will come a time when no one wants to hear about the one you lost, what you did together, what they did, or what they thought. It is harsh but true. Harsh because you will feel offended in some way or feel like they are showing disrespect, but they are not. You can only say, "They would have loved this; they would have done this; they would have . . ." so many times before it loses its power and begins to have a negative impact. You cannot live in the past.

This means, over time, fewer and fewer people will remember those key dates: day of birth, day of marriage, day of death, and many more and a new type of loneliness begins. Your life should be about using your past to manage the present in order to build a future. If you haven't learned how to adapt to the present and move on into the future, you will actually dishonor what you had together.

How you share your history, your life together, will prevent that and give you the tools to keep on doing what you have been doing. A great way to honor that person is to do just that. And the most important person to see this fact is you. It really doesn't matter how many know how or what your past is contributing to the present to create a future. The ones who need to know already do, and they will recognize the presence of your loved one in what is happening. And whether or not they state it, you will know they understand.

So where will you live? How will you reveal that to others?

# Better

Often when a person dies after a serious accident or long and difficult sickness the comment comes, "It is better." The ones who say this are expressing a common thought that in some way the death of the person is a good thing. The point of the comment being that somehow this knowledge will ease the pain of the loss.

There are a number of similar statements that follow this idea: "They are in a better place." "Everything will be better." But what does this truly mean?

Recently, I was talking to a friend who was dealing with the concept of better. In this case, it was not about the death of a loved one. For this friend, the issue was how to care for a family member as a disease slowly took away the person's capacity to think, to care for themselves, and created needs and demands beyond the ability of my friend to meet.

It had been a difficult day and out came the question, "Wouldn't it be better if . . . ?" I heard the anger in the voice, not just from the frustration of the day, but anger at themselves for even thinking about placing their loved one in a care facility because it might be better. We talked about this later, and the reality that better is a moving target and there are multiple layers to what better is and means. I will come back to that later.

This was the third time in recent years that the idea of better has become a significant issue for me and those close to me. The first time was in dealing with long-term care for my mother who had a form of Alzheimer's that completely removed all memory, past and present.

We had to decide if it would be better for my brother and his wife to care for her or if it would be better for my mother to be placed in a care facility. In the end the better was placement in a care facility that dealt with people with Alzheimer's.

The second situation was the death of my wife after a thirteen-year battle with breast cancer. Her death, when it came, came quickly, and many made the comment that now she was in a better place. Up until days before her death, this was not even something we considered. She was handling treatment well and for the most part, could do whatever she wanted.

Each time we approached a change in her condition, the treatment not working, there was always another option. In the back of our minds we knew that one day this would not be true, but until then better was always, another treatment, and being able to recover once again.

Then came the day when better wasn't happening. This time things just got worse until another better happened. Actually, two betters came into view. The obvious one was that she was now in a better place and no longer would be affected by the cancer.

The other hid in the background for a while but finally made itself known. It was better this way. She did not suffer a lot; it all happened quickly. This better can be hard to face. We don't see the better because we don't feel better. We may, in an intellectual way, see the better, but emotionally we don't feel the better because the person is gone.

People will come and tell stories about others they have known who suffered a slow and agonizing death. They think that somehow by telling the story, you will see the blessing, the better, and so feel better. It rarely works, at least at the deeper emotional level where grief is tearing the person apart.

In time, this better is understood and brings a sense of peace. In the same way, the comment, "They are in a better place," is only understood and accepted in a superficial way. Like the first better comment, the loss is too deep to really allow one to do more than acknowledge the possibility of it being better for the one who has died and for you. That is because there remains a deeper emotion of grief that says, "How can it be better when we are no longer together? How can it be better as I find myself trying to carry on and do all the things that used to be done by two?" In time, something that varies for each person, this better will bring comfort. It is better because they are now whole. It is better because I am learning to live again.

(Of course, this only works if in fact the person was a Christian and there is no doubt of their eternal home. If not, then these words will not bring a sense of better. They are gone with no chance of doing what needed to be done to be better. There will be incredible pain, regret, and guilt because there is no possibility of better. But that is an area for another time. But I needed to mention it.)

There is a third better that may appear over time. This is not an easy one to see and even more difficult to accept. It is not always present because not every situation will create the environment needed for this better to exist. Certain conditions have to be in place or there will be no need to look at this concept and wrestle with its reality.

This better is tied to a couple of what ifs. What if the latest treatment had worked but their level of health and quality of life diminished? What if all this meant the need to make major changes in plans, the nature of one's work and lifestyle, and one's relationships with other people? What if the disease progressed further and created greater restrictions and suffering? These are not pleasant issues to face or consider.

When this better comes and people talk about how it is better they didn't suffer, it can be difficult to see that, what they really meant was, it was better they left when they did so that your life would be better. If not handled correctly, this better can open the door for coldness and anger to settle in. The reaction to this better can be very negative and loaded with emotion. How dare you say, "It was better that they die and leave me?" How can you be so cold and unfeeling? Who gave you the right to say what is better for them or me? And on it goes.

But there is a reality here that must be faced at some point. In every situation like this, there will come a day when it is better. Better for the person who died, and better for those left behind. Better because it means the end of suffering for both people and because it allows for new possibilities and life because it allows the one left behind to recover and do what could not be done or would not be possible until that moment came.

I have slowly begun to see it. If my wife had slowly weakened and required more and more care, then my life would have needed to change, my activities, my schedule, my focus, and more would need to be set aside to care for her, and knowing my wife she would have suffered at another level. She would not want to be the reason for limiting our level of involvement in ministry. The more limits her state caused, the more pain it would bring to her. This would be another kind of cancer and not be part of the promise of God to have a plan to prosper her and us as a couple.

While we never talked about it, I believe that deep in us this was something we were aware of, and it made understanding at this level possible for me. It also paved the way for the transition to this better to occur less painfully.

The third situation is from the story above, of a friend who is dealing with knowing what is better. The struggle, in this case, is somewhat like that of my mother. When does what is better for me and better for my loved one become the same thing? The struggle here is a little different. With my mother, she had no knowledge of what was happening. At least conscious awareness she could express. At first, she knew something was wrong and became frustrated. Over time, this awareness disappeared.

For my friend, their spouse knows what is happening. So far, they have done well at making the needed changes to keep life running at a reasonable level. The problem is that the better keeps shifting. At first, it meant changing jobs so the spouse could function and feel useful. Then it meant realizing that it was not possible to keep on working but that there was still a need to have meaningful activity. Small jobs around the house, adult daycare trips and events, and activities with friends who understood what was happening. We were part of several of these, and we enjoyed the time together and helping our friend provide the better in the moment.

Now things are shifting again. To have a better life now means downsizing. My friend is sorting, selling, and donating the stuff of their life. Once that is done, they are selling their house and moving into an apartment to make life simpler or better. This has not come without stress because there are two different betters at play. What is better for the one struggling with a deteriorating disease, and what is better for the one watching and caring for that person?

The family has been very supportive in this process, but still, there is this stress, the tension between better for me and better for my spouse, and better for family and loved ones. It was this that caused an angry response and pain. A key aspect of this was the person's concept of the timeline involved. Just how much time was involved and how their concept of when things needed to happen and done was shifting. My friend is very organized and structured, and when the ability to control the environment slips away, better becomes undefinable and fuzzy.

Now the struggle was clearly between better for me and better for my spouse. My friend was so glad for my call that day. It allowed her to freely express the struggle with no fear of judgment, no fear of criticism. We have that kind of relationship. And that is a critical aspect of how one handles what is better. Because in each of the betters, the final question is the same. How is this better? How is it better for me and for the other person who is involved, whether it involves death or dealing with a debilitating disease?

I must be honest: there is no simple answer or quick fix. I wish there were, but from what I have learned, no matter how well we handle the better there will always be a struggle with various ideas: Am I being selfish? Am I being insensitive? Am I weak and unable to act and do what is better?

How this plays out will vary with every individual. Why? Because there are far too many variables in every situation. Nature of death, nature of the illness, nature of the relationship, nature of . . .

I am still learning what better means. The good news is that I have found a few persons willing to listen to me as I express what I am learning.

Listen without judgment. Listen without assuming they really understand. Listen knowing I need to talk and express my struggle. Listen because, without realizing it, they too are struggling with the same issue from another perspective and need to know how I am processing it.

Is it better? In time, it will be, and I will want the better. I will see the better. And finally, I will live a new kind of better. One I could not see before.

# Alone and Lonely

At some point in the grieving process you will begin to deal with the fact that you are alone now, because the person, your mate, is not there. You come home and there is no one to greet you. There is no one to share with what is happening in your life, no one to sit down and eat a meal with. The space next to you on the sofa, in the bed, and many other places is vacant. At the same time, you may think that you are becoming lonely. But are you really either of these? These words may appear similar or related, but in many ways, they are quite different. And how you understand and deal with them will be critical because at a certain level they are both true and you will never fully overcome their effect.

I have learned in my life that you can be in a crowd of people, not alone, and still be lonely. You can walk down the hall of your school, where you work, and be among people and be very lonely.

On the other hand, you can find yourself alone, by yourself, and not be lonely. You are standing in a large empty hall, in an open field, or even in yourself with no one present and not be lonely.

So, what do these two words mean, especially when the one who filled your life and empty spaces is now gone? What is happening, and how does that affect you and your life as you move forward in learning to live without your spouse or other loved one?

I am beginning to understand more what they mean based on several factors that have been part of my life.

The first is from when I was in high school and college, I learned about being lonely. I was part of large groups of people, took part in activities with others, and went to classes with fellow classmen, in other words rarely alone. Yet I was lonely.

Lonely was not about how many people were around me, but about not having someone in my life that cared about me or wanted me to care about them. That reality taught me that lonely is a two-sided coin. The head's side was that you have no one who is interested in what is happening in your life. And I am not talking about parents and family. They are usually interested, but that sometimes intensifies the sense of loneliness. It is like this, why don't others have the same interest in my life as they do in the lives of others?

This loneliness comes from the fact that, in a way, parents and family members are expected to be interested, at least to a certain point. The level of this loneliness depends on the nature of their interest. Many parents are generally interested in the life and activities of their children. This softens the impact of the other level of loneliness, the lack of interest of others. But if they are only interested because your success or activities fill some need in them, then their interest will intensify your sense of loneliness. They are living vicariously via your success in order to fulfill some empty spot in their lives from the past or present. If this is true, then the sense of loneliness can be more intense when you are with them. Not alone but lonely.

The next worst scenario is when they don't care but are simply acting out our expectations of their concept of the role of parents, the expectations of others for those who are parents, and are doing so because just because. This causes intense barriers and mistrust to any attempt to praise you or take part at any level in what is your life.

At the worst level, they don't care at all. This type of lack of concern makes loneliness incredibly intense and makes it difficult to believe anyone can care about you.

Each of these levels has a direct impact on our sense of loneliness and how a person reacts to the interest of others.

It is true, that interest by parents and lack of interest by others creates a discordant situation. This can often highlight and intensify loneliness. It can create a false feeling that everything is all right, and the person can manage the sense of loneliness created by the lack of interest and connection with others. For a while, it does work, but in time that lack will make itself known and strongly impact a person's sense of worth and self-confidence. Something that is masked because no one is interested, which results in the feeling that the person shouldn't bother others.

I know this effect all too well and have no intention of going further into this. What I have shared should be enough to explain this side of the coin.

The flip side is the inability to show interest and be concerned about others by the one who is dealing with loneliness. It is just as treacherous and complicated as the other side. Maybe more so.

The range of options is from a complete disregard for others, their feelings, and anything that has to do with them, to attempts at showing interest in those around them, because if the lonely person does this, then maybe, just maybe, others will do the same for me. In the extreme version of the first, the person often creates a prickly shell around them so that anyone who comes near becomes a target of anger and other emotional actions to keep them away and maintain the reality that the person doesn't care.

The other extreme may appear open and altruistic, but it is difficult to maintain such behavior. It is difficult to care about others when they don't care about you. And it carries the danger of feeding the selfish behavior of others who gladly receive the involvement of the person who is lonely without the issue of being accountable. Accountable for the debt they are creating by receiving such attention with no thought of reciprocity. In time, that environment will create another form of loneliness, the flip side of the coin.

The lonely person invests in the lives of others and tries to get others to care for them but never develops relationships, and so becomes isolated and dependent. In time, they will finally realize this, but they are now dependent on the emotional gifts and care of others.

Giving and giving with nothing or no one to help recharge one's emotional batteries comes at a cost. The cost is loneliness and isolation. The person tries to care about others, but they don't return the care, and isolation sets in. As a result, they find themselves in the group but isolated and lonely because they really are not part of the group.

That is a very brief look at the issue of loneliness.

Being alone and by yourself is not the same. There are many good reasons for being alone. Many times, when being alone is necessary, even required, to care for oneself. The danger here is in not finding the time to be alone or in avoiding it because of what being alone may represent or mean.

We need to be alone and are encouraged to take time to meditate, read the Bible, and learn to listen. We need the aloneness to better understand who we are, what we have, and what we need. To be honest, I am sitting here alone thinking about this topic to gain a better perspective on what has happened in my life. My wife died and I am alone. At least that is how I feel. But getting caught up in what I feel can be misleading.

I may be physically alone, but am I truly alone? For the lonely person being alone is negative and happens even when in the midst of a crowd. Loneliness generates the feeling of being alone everywhere. And for that person actually being by themselves is often less stressful because there is no constant reminder of what they are experiencing.

But back to the question, am I really alone? That depends on what is causing this to happen and what my life is filled with.

Let me explain. If I am alone at this moment, it may only be in a physical sense. Yes, I stand, sit, eat, and sleep in the house by myself. But I am not completely alone because we raised a family and they care about me. We developed friends and many other contacts who are praying and keeping a watchful eye on what was happening in our world. This has not changed, and in some ways it is more intense now than before. People are still praying and interested in my life.

So, while one may be alone physically, they are not completely alone. They may have many people who are interested in their lives and still want that person to be part of their lives. The hard part in this is the transition that must take place from depending on one key person to provide or be the channel of that emotional and physical contact, to learning how to let others combine to provide a reasonable replacement for what was lost.

Reasonable in that, if one is honest, it is because no one can replace the connection that existed between a husband and wife in a good marriage. Note, I say good, great and perfect don't really exist. *We* may say it is so, but that does not help in making the transition. Having said that, there is no combination of relations, children, family, and friends that can replace that. And that is not a goal to seek if one is going to deal with being alone in a healthy manner.

In this situation, being alone, when managed correctly, allows the person to gain a clear perspective on what they had and allow others to enter their life to build a reasonable structure to provide for much of what is missing. Much because there is no replacement for the private chats, the cuddling, the walking down the beach hand in hand, and snuggling in bed. Much of which involved no verbal communication or affirmation but provided a profound depth of intimacy and responsiveness. You know what the other is feeling without needing to speak.

If the person does not learn to accept the involvement of others and deal with the fact that they cannot fully replace what has been lost, then they risk moving from just being alone into being lonely. And all that was described above becomes the background for what could happen here in this situation.

Lonely and alone are two different concepts, but when they become united, it is dangerous emotionally and relationally. To avoid this, each person will need to find appropriate ways to communicate what is happening. How this is done will vary with every person: Writing letters to yourself until you can share them with others; writing notes, poems, and comments to a few close friends and family. Sometimes these notes may have to be held in reserve because they may be struggling with the same issues.

For example, when one parent dies, the one left behind is alone and wants to reach out because it will help him or her but one or more of the children are not ready yet. This can be a challenge if not handled correctly. Acting too soon will create anger, frustration, and pain mainly for the child that is struggling. If you wait too long, other issues can begin to develop: a sense of abandonment, a sense of failure, for example. So, writing letters and notes to be held in reserve for a later, more appropriate time, will be vital. Some may even keep a diary that will be shared at the right time.

No matter what a person does, it is important to find a way to communicate the aloneness so that loneliness will not become too great an issue. And truthfully, even when everything is done correctly, there will be a sense of loneliness just because no one has experienced what you have experienced, and it is almost impossible to explain, even to those who have lost what you lost. There is always something different that makes it unique to you.

So yes, I am alone but not alone. At times I feel lonely, but I know that is only a temporary feeling because there are people who care.

# Stages of Grief

I have been reflecting on what people call the stages of grief. The terms often used are actually from a study by Kübler-Ross on what happens when a person is diagnosed with a terminal illness or a life-altering accident. They are popularly known as the five stages of grief and are a good description of what happens emotionally when a person receives the diagnosis that they are terminally ill or will never recover from a debilitating accident.

When applied to addressing terminal illness or incapacitating illness, these stages are seen as sequential. What is not often realized is that a person may pass through them several times as they deal with different types and levels of loss. But do these stages relate to loss that results from the death of a loved one?

First let's get a brief idea of what the stages are and then consider if they can be applied to the loss of a loved one through death, whether sudden or anticipated.

1.  Denial: disbelief that the diagnosis is true or is in some way mistaken. The person clings to a false and preferable reality.
2.  Anger: this is what happens when denial doesn't work. It involves frustration and anger, which can be directed toward others and involves the question of, *Why me?* Often in the process, there is an attempt to place blame on others.
3.  Bargaining: at this point, a new hope emerges that somehow the cause of grief can be avoided or overcome. People will "negotiate with God" for more time so they can attend a special event. Sometimes, the bargaining includes promises to change if more time is given. It can also include bargaining to enter experimental treatment programs and the use of risky and unproven treatments.
4.  Depression: this begins to develop when the denial, anger, and bargaining don't work. The feeling is that I am going to die so why bother to try to live and care about what is happening. At this point, the person is confronted with their mortality and inability to effect any change in the diagnosis.
5.  Acceptance: at this point, the person accepts the reality of the situation. A sense of calm enters, and they embrace what lies ahead.

These stages affect both the person who is diagnosed with a terminal illness or life-altering illness and those nearest to them. Both groups go through this process but at differing rates and with different focuses. In fact, they can go through the process multiple times because there exists more than one type of loss. (If you want to read more, then it would be a good idea to find material that deals specifically with this process.)

The death of a loved one does not fit this process. Let me be clear: I am not talking about what may have happened leading up to the death. What I am talking about fits the examples below:

1. Sudden death because of an accident or catastrophic event.
2. Death after processing all the grief issues related to terminal illness.

In these cases, some of the above will apply but not in the way one would expect. Let us consider each of the stages and see how they might apply to the death of a loved one.

## *Denial*

There is no way to deny the death. Although some may say, "I won't believe they are dead until I see their body." And on rare occasions, that may be a valid comment (for example, those who are lost during war and are listed as missing in action). To prevent this denial from continuing, we have funerals and open coffins to establish without a doubt that the person has died and will not be returning.

But even as I say this, I realize that there is a manner in which people work hard to deny, in an emotional way, the death and absence of a loved one. They refuse to let go of the things that represent the relationship. The clothing, the memorabilia, and other items. The house will be filled with the stuff of that person. They may go as far as to create a shrine to the person using these items to create a sense of the presence of the person. They may create a spot in the home where photos and personal items are placed to maintain the memory of the person.

The closets remain full of the clothing, the jewelry and other personal items are kept and put on display. Memorabilia and gifts are kept and put on display. The ways these things develop and are used to delay further loss can be very creative. New rituals are developed to maintain memories and the presence of that one who died. Or the old patterns are followed meticulously to maintain the aura of the presence of the one who has died in their world.

The most subtle one for me is the concept that the one who has died is now watching over my life and actions. That in some way she is still actively part of my world. I am not talking about the comment that goes like this, "Nancy (my wife) would have enjoyed doing this with us." Or a similar comment. That is an honest memory of the person. But the idea that somehow they are watching, and we must be careful that what we do makes them happy and does not offend. Or the idea that in some way they are still active in our life and helping us in some way. That is a form of denial.

Biblically this does not occur. No scripture supports that idea. Some might use the cloud of witnesses in Hebrews 12:1, but that is about the number of people who have already passed this way and provide testimony about what faith in God means. The Bible never suggests that there are disembodied spirits watching us. In fact, it talks about how they have entered into the presence of God and their heavenly rest (He 4:9). They suffer no more. For me, it would be incredibly painful for them to have to watch us sin and possibly fail to be saved.

But at some point, this denial must stop. At least the public nature of it must change, and the person must move on, so to speak. At some point, it will be necessary to let go of the stuff. Not everything. That would be the opposite extreme of denial, to act like the person no longer has a place in one's life, to act like the memories and relationship must be completely excised as if it was another type of cancer.

This type of denial exists. The person doesn't want to hear the name of the one who died. The person doesn't want to go anywhere they went together or be involved in an activity they shared in. This often involves getting rid of everything connected with the one who has died, relocation to a new place, and in a way starting a new life. Contact with friends is restricted to avoid dealing with the loss. This is denial as well. If there are no reminders, then I don't have to deal with the death.

The reality is that in both situations there is no denial of the death of the person but more a denial or unwillingness to deal with that loss. In the one, it is, "I won't let them go," and the other is, "I don't want to remember anything of them that would cause me pain and grief." The better goal is not to deny the loss but learn to live with the loss, to understand what that loss means and what I will gain as I learn what it means.

One more thing to keep in mind. This may not happen at all. There will be no denial which may result in enshrinement or disconnecting. And it may not happen when the death actually occurs but may develop later as a response to other losses. Less and less people wanting to talk about how things used to be can result in creating a shrine to hold on to what has been lost. Or too many people always reminding the person of what has been lost resulting in disconnecting and avoidance.

## Anger

The second idea of anger is very real. For a more detailed discussion of this topic read the material in the previous sections on anger. But as in the areas above, it can occur at different levels and at different times. It can be directed at those around us and it can be directed at ourselves. What is interesting is that it has no relationship to overcoming denial. It is about the loss and its impact on my life. And what triggers the anger may have nothing to do with what has happened but what is happening or may happen in the future.

At the moment: why didn't they do more to prevent their death?

- Facing the death: Why did you die now?
- Happening: I don't want to deal with all of this
- Happening: Why do people avoid me?
- Later: Why doesn't anyone talk about my wife anymore?
- Later: It is not fair that I must live alone.

Again, none of this may occur, or all of it may – but rarely all at once. It all depends on the person and the support group they have.

## Bargaining

The next one is bargaining. In death, there is no bargaining. The person is dead, and you cannot make a bargain to bring them back. Although people do make the attempt. But it is in a past tense form. Why didn't you take me instead of them? But that is more anger speaking.

I recognize that several people were raised from the dead in the Bible. A key idea to keep in mind is that usually there was no request made that they be raised to life. What commonly occurred were comments related to if you had only come sooner, they would not have died. While a person was sick, there may have been bargaining, but after they die, not usually. Okay, maybe when a great or important person dies, people may wish they could have died in their place, but that again is after the fact.

Am I making sense? Once death comes, we don't, can't, bargain related to the death. But we may bargain related to the pain and sorrow that comes afterward. This may be true if there are serious issues of guilt and regret to be dealt with. Bargaining may take this form: "I will make this change or do this, if you will take away the pain and guilt that I am experiencing as a result of this loss."

In some cases, the bargaining may be in reverse: I deserve this pain and the results of my guilt, and I deserve more. Lay it all on me so others will not have to suffer as a result of what happened. I deserve all that I am getting and more.

But, in general, there is no concept of bargaining when dealing with grief as a result of the death of a loved one.

There does exist one other possibility: A person may use the death of a person as a bargaining chip in controlling the actions of others. It may other forms: "You owe me," or "If you really cared about the person you would . . ." But this is not really bargaining in relation to the loss and its impact on my life and how I will live from now on.

## *Depression*

This one is truly a part of the process of grief, and like anger, it is real and must be dealt with. Mostly, it is about not being able to live without the person who has died. This feeling is strongest when one spouse loses their partner, or a child loses a parent. For the child, a lot will depend on the age of the child and the nature of the relationship. To be honest, losing my mother of ninety years of age, who has suffered from severe Alzheimer's, will not cause this response. But a teenager losing a parent may feel this way.

Depression comes as one deals with the reality of being alone. At least physically. Depression also comes as one deals with the emotional loss of that person who understands and fills the blank spaces. Depression comes as day-after-day life must be lived without that person's help and presence. The key here is to find ways to manage the severity of it. That is because it is impossible to avoid any of these realities. Those who do will suffer. You can only maintain a false reality for a while, and then it will crash in on you.

And again, as in the others, there is no knowing when it will come. In fact, it may come, go away, and then come back in a different way. The depression of the days and weeks after the death will be one time frame. That may pass, and then depression sets in as the reality of living alone sets in.

That may pass, and then the struggle with fading memories or the fading presence of the person. And one more can come much later if the person considers remarrying or establishing a relationship that would in effect replace what was lost. This can cause another type of depression.

I hate to repeat myself, but depression may have no relationship whatsoever with denial, anger, or bargaining. It is also not dependent on whether they have occurred. In fact, I can think of one possibility where depression can be the source of anger: Anger at myself for allowing myself to become depressed over the loss.

The problem is more complex than can be covered in this short space. Different aspects of this issue are touched on in other sections of the material.

## *Acceptance*

I think this one may be the most complicated of them all. There are so many aspects to this. It exists in a strange continuum of realities. The person is gone but is very present in every aspect of who I am and how I live. The person is gone, and I have learned to live without them and have forged a new way of living and coping. The person is gone, and I am creating a new world that doesn't include them.

How do I explain the vast variety of ways in which people accept the death of a spouse?

Maybe two extremes will serve.

I know a person whose wife had been severely ill with cancer for more than ten years. Besides that, the wife had a serious problem emotionally as a result of being bipolar. They loved each other, and he lovingly cared for her year after year. What is interesting is that as her life neared an end, she actively sought a new wife for him. They even invited at least one to their house so he could meet her.

I found this to be very strange, and I wondered about the emotional stress and issues that may arise in such a situation. He, in fact, married one of the ladies he and his wife had considered and is now very happy in his new marriage. And according to family members, he is doing extremely well emotionally. He found a way to be released from the past and move on.

It will be interesting to see and hear how he does in the years ahead in processing his loss. But clearly, he has accepted the situation and created a new way of living to cope with the struggle and loss of his wife.

I am at the other extreme. My world is filled with the presence of my wife. I am who I am as a person because of our years of marriage. And while I can care for all of my needs without her, I know that whatever I do in the future must take into account the fact that, truthfully, in my life and work I cannot avoid her presence and impact. To do so would be emotionally destructive.

As a result, I am beginning to understand a little about how some who have lost a spouse never remarry or take years before they can do so. There just isn't room for another person in their life. Even though she is not physically present, she permeates my world. And it is positive because that presence gives me the strength to move forward and adapt or accept the new parameters of my life.

I am also beginning to understand why some remarry rather quickly. Their dependence exists at a different level and can only be dealt with by the presence of another person in their life.

Some can live successfully and happily in their loss and others cannot do so without another person near to help them, someone nearer than a friend or family member.

Acceptance does not mean there will be no anger about something in the future. It does not mean there will never be a problem with times of depression. It does not grow out of overcoming denial or anger or depression. In this structure, the ability to accept what has happened provides a solid foundation to prevent denial, to deal with anger, and to overcome the times of depression.

Well, this has been interesting. When I began this section, I was planning on showing how some of the five stages of grief don't apply to death. And in the normal understanding of the process of grief as related to facing one's death, they don't. They are not sequential. Yet they do exist, but in ways that are unique to the issue of death and with other focuses.

This means that three of these are part of the process, anger, depression, and acceptance. The other two may become part of the process depending on how we handle the loss, how stable we are emotionally, whether we have had a healthy relationship with the one we have lost, and of course, the nature of our support group.

And as we have seen, there is no sequence, no order, in what happens. Think about it: Anger can lead to denial. Bargaining can result in anger. Depression can cause a desire to enter into denial by creating a shrine or excising the person from our memory. None of them opens the way to acceptance, but clearly, acceptance helps deal with all of the others. Besides, there are several other issues that cannot be considered under this concept of five stages or aspects of loss.

There is a key issue in just how intense we experience any of these and whether we handle them correctly or lose control. It has to do with how we have processed the challenges of life before we arrive at the day of death. That will determine how, and if, we struggle with any of these issues and several others that are not included in the five stages. You see, I am discovering there is much more going on than simply passing through a prescribed set of stages. Grief doesn't work that way, because grief is a personal experience and much more complex than can be covered in something like five stages.

# Intimacy and Its Loss

Well here goes a topic most men steer clear of, and yet can't avoid. When your spouse dies, you will realize what it is, even if you deny being the emotional sort, and you will hurt because of what you have lost.

Before we get too far into this and lest someone say I am getting too personal, you need to realize there are different areas of intimacy. And I am dealing with them all, and sometimes all at once. So a list of key areas will help to guide this material: (1) emotional intimacy, (2) spiritual intimacy, and (3) the big one, physical intimacy.

**Emotional intimacy** is where we will start. The easy one, right? Who am I kidding? Emotional intimacy is not an easy subject. Men are not supposed to be emotional. But no matter how you hide it, disguise it, ignore it, or avoid it, you are emotional. And you need the intimacy of another emotional being, or you will go crazy. You can overcome a lot of stress in your life as long as you don't lose this.

Let me make it simple: You need someone who is emotionally connected to you. My wife was just that, an emotional connection. She opened my eyes and heart to emotions and how they affect people and how to respond to others. Now I am not an overly emotional person. You know, the men don't cry type of stuff. I grew up in a Scandinavian environment, with the cold feelings of a Viking. That is overstating it a bit, but it is a part of who I am.

With my wife at my side, I could be intimate with my emotions. Not that I got all gushy and teary-eyed and loved watching those romantic Christmas movies produced by Hallmark. But I could let down my defenses and be honest about what was happening inside. And even if I didn't explain it well in words, she knew what I was feeling.

That is the best of all worlds. Experiencing the emotions and enjoying the freedom that comes when they are expressed, by words, a gesture, or being together in silence. Now I know my wife loved it when I used words. You can only do so much interpretation of gestures, sighs, and other grunting and groaning. But those words will have little meaning if there is no emotional intimacy.

Really, when your wife has to say, "I just want to hear you say it," it is already too late or almost too late to say it. You are going to have to do a lot of stuff in the way of actions to prove your emotional intimacy for those words to matter. And I am not talking about the nice stuff you do because you did something you shouldn't have done, or you forgot to do what they expected, that is debt recovery. I am referring to what you do because you want to do it.

Are you understanding what I am saying? The one you just lost provided all of that, and now it is all gone. There is no one to look at who will know what emotions are running around in your head and heart. That person who could smile at you and bring peace, calm, and so much joy is gone and there are no more emotional outlets at this level.

There is no one to listen to you as you talk about the emotions happening in your life. The frustration at work, satisfaction in some project, or anything where having a person who knows you intimately, at the level of your emotions, provides the outlet you need.

And you no longer have someone who trusts you with all the above in their life. No one you can listen to and encourage. No one to smile at, frown with, and help with the hurts and successes that emotions bring into their world and yours.

All of that is gone. And when you realize it, you . . . well, you may break down into some of those emotional responses you used to have such great control over. A control made possible because of the emotional intimacy and trust you had and is now gone.

**Spiritual intimacy** is another area. This one is probably a little more obvious. You could read the word of God, pray, and study devotionals together. If your level of intimacy was growing and maturing, that meant you had someone who wanted to know what you thought about the sermon of the day, a scripture they had read, or a challenge they were facing.

You as well could share it in the same way. She may not agree with you, but she would not criticize you unduly and was willing to take the time to think it through with you until you were able as a couple to come to a reasonable position. One that allowed both of you to be right if there was a difference. One that strengthened each other when there was agreement.

I know how important this is at a very personal level. When we met, I told my then-girlfriend that if we were to become serious in our relationship, she had to agree to go with me as a missionary, something she had never considered before. She said yes, love does that, and I believed her, love does that as well.

We had some struggles as we worked through what all that meant and how it could/would affect our life. When there is spiritual intimacy, there is space for all that to happen without personal attack or criticism. Intimacy means we work together to find God's solution and then help each other in applying what has been learned. It is not about who wins or has the better argument. It is two people working together to understand God's direction.

There is also the fact that when two people are intimate at a spiritual level, they also help each other see what the other might not see. People have different perspectives, and intimacy allows for this reality and encourages it. You read the same truth and each person gains something different, which then becomes the basis of creating a better understanding of what was studied.

Yes, I know this is what should happen in any Bible study. The difference is with couples there is a unique level of knowledge and relationship that can't exist in a group Bible study. A couple has access to much more personal information about each other and so can take the lessons learned to a different level. And they are with each other all the time, watching and encouraging each other all the time. This can be dangerous if there is discord, but incredibly powerful if there is true intimacy in their spiritual relationship with God and each other.

You won't realize how much you depend on and need this, nor how much you desire it until it is missing and, with the death of a spouse, gone. There is no one to pray with that doesn't need more information. There is no one to talk with that doesn't need more details in order to understand where you are coming from. There is no one to test your ideas on and to encourage you as you learn to trust God and follow His direction.

Yep, no one to read the devotional to or listen as they read. I am still using a devotional we were using before my wife died. It is good material, but my spiritual partner in the journey is gone. She had unique insights, and occasionally I think I might see it from her eyes and heart, but it is only a guess. Those special times of spiritual intimacy are gone, and I am the poorer for it.

**Physical intimacy** is the one we all are wondering about. And to start off, I am not going to explore just sexual intimacy. Physical intimacy is about so much more and includes hugging, holding hands, kissing, snuggling, and yes sexual intimacy. They are all part of this area.

We need to not just know that person is near but feel it in so many situations. We need the hugs as an affirmation that the person knows we are there, and they are both pleased and encouraged by it. Many books have been written on the value of a hug.

Holding hands is about making a connection. It communicates so much. I am here with you because I want to be with you. I am here to support you in what you are doing. I am here because I enjoy being with you, and I want others to know that fact.

Kissing has so much power to do so many things. It is an act of confirmation of our love. It is the act that seals and proves our words of forgiveness. It is an act that is used to finalize a promise made. And it just feels so good in so many ways. It can be as simple as a peck on the cheek, on the hand, head, even foot if you wish. Or it can be as profound as that kiss that binds a couple in love and is repeated over and over throughout the marriage. Long and passionate kisses that don't care who is looking.

Those kisses grant incredible power to the marriage. They mend areas damaged by our mistakes. They tell us that nothing is impossible as long as we are together. They confirm the promise we made to love each other no matter what happens.

Now we come to snuggling. You might think it should come before the kissing stuff. But I disagree. I know because I have had a lot of experience with the snuggling stuff, of actually sitting close because you want to, even though there is plenty of room to spread out and sit. My wife was a snuggler. She would often call me to sit with her. And before I knew it, we were snuggling.

With a kiss, you have to come up for air once in a while. With a snuggle, there is no time limit. With a kiss, you have to do a little work to have your lips meet properly so you don't cause discomfort. But with snuggling, there are no such problems. And you can snuggle in so many ways, each providing a profoundly deep connection.

I am not interested in what position works best. The point is when two people are snuggling there are a couple of things happening. The most important is contentment. We are happy and pleased and so just enjoy the wonder of being together. There is another, and that is a sense of protection and security that is experienced. It doesn't matter if there is any real danger or need to keep each other warm. Snuggling or cuddling (for those who don't understand snuggling) does wonders for both. Ask any parent who cuddles with a fearful child or one who feels chilled, just what happens.

Now take it to the level of a husband and wife who are snuggling. The contentment, the sense of security and warmth that exists in this act of intimacy. Oh, and did I mention it allows you to be vulnerable without judgment or repercussions?

And finally, there is sexual intimacy. Not just sex but intimacy. Knowing the needs of each other and satisfying them at one of the most profound levels possible. Again, without fear, guilt, or any other negative emotions. And that is all I am going to say about that.

But now it is all gone. There are no hugs, no kisses. There are no times of snuggling and sexual intimacy. The person is gone, and you can't go find a hug, get a kiss. The chair, sofa, swing, whatever you used for snuggling is empty. No one is there to sit with, lay with, and just be at peace. And the bed is empty.

All you have now are memories, and they can satisfy for a while, and then the reality comes. You thought you knew what it meant to be alone. Your wife died. You didn't need anyone to remind you about that, but they did. Over time, slowly the conversations shifted because they knew you didn't need another reminder. A few, those who know you and have permission, will ask how you are doing. You answer them, and usually they are satisfied with your answer, if you are doing okay.

But there is no way to avoid the other reminders: the empty house, the empty seat in the car, the conversation with yourself, the meals alone that you prepare. On and on the list goes.

Emotionally, spiritually, and physically alone. And day after day filled with reminders. Over time, the impact will lessen, but the reminders won't go away. You will need to deal with them and find reasonable substitutes in each area. I say reasonable because there are also unreasonable, even dangerous, options for each one.

It is not easy, and to be honest I don't think I will find another person like my wife. I am learning that I am going to have to depend more and more on God to fill the gaps and bring others my way to give me a moment, a glimpse, a brief encounter that is enough to keep me moving forward and dealing, step by step, with the loss of intimacy in my life.

# The Price of Grief

It has now been almost a year and a half since my wife died, and I think I can now comment on something I mentioned in another section. It was about how long does one carry out certain actions related to *in memory of.* I was concerned about how some people, in my thoughts, don't seem to get beyond the need or desire, you decide, to recall, reflect on, remember their loss.

Here is what I have come to learn. Whether you begin a ritual of remembrance or don't, there is a price that you will pay. Your grief will exact it in one form or another. There is no escaping this reality. You have lost someone very close to you, someone who was so much a part of your life that their departure leaves you struggling with the loss at so many levels and in so many ways.

At first, the price is evident. You are having to learn how to live without your wife. Then as time passes, and you have adjusted to some degree, another event occurs. You are alone; you are interacting with others, and they remind you of what you have lost, your wife. It doesn't really matter how well they knew you as a couple. They will convey their condolences or sadness or apologize in some way, not that it was their fault; it is just how people respond. And you pay.

But that is all normal and to be expected. It is part of the first year or so, and then we move into another reality and another layer of paying. It is most evident in special events that happen either annually or in certain unique one-time events.

The most obvious are birthdays and anniversaries as well as special times that were shared and developed into annual events. Things like family reunions, Thanksgiving, Christmas celebrations, and more. Each of them becomes a reminder of what is missing and exacts a price emotionally. How much these events exact will depend on several factors: (1) how you handle those events at a personal level; (2) how the people involved deal with it and react to your presence minus your spouse; (3) the level of importance given to the event as a couple, at all cost or only as possible?; and (4) how close you were to the people involved.

If the price is too high, you begin to make them private. You don't remind people of the significance of the day. You don't celebrate your birthday or hers or other events because it just reminds you of your loss. You don't attend those special events because it is just too costly emotionally.

But you will pay because your absence will create a response. The next time you see them, they will make a point to tell you about your absence. Or you may no longer receive invitations since they already know you are not coming and why. In this case, you pay and make them pay instead of you paying. Your absence becomes a powerful reminder to them of what has happened. (They may say something like, "We haven't seen him since his wife died.")

Then there are the events that are once in a lifetime. Marriage of a child, birth of a grandchild, graduation of grown children, move to another city or place, and on the list goes. Events that cause people to say things like, "She would have loved to be here; she would have loved to hold the new grandchild; she would have . . .; it is so sad that she could not be here to see this and be part of what is happening."

There are levels of intensity in this type of cost. For the children of a parent who has died, it can be very intense emotionally. The birth of a new grandchild, and so on. There are two ways that the price is exacted. Others exact it from you without thinking that you are there and dealing with this cost at a very personal level or, before others have the chance, you exact it of them. You make them pay emotionally so that you can gain emotional change for your bank. The one is a normal process, the other is a dangerous way to live. and people may decide not to invite or include you in those events because the price is too high.

I see it because every time I see my kids, grandkids, and do something with them, that reality is present, and I have to pay a price to be there. If I don't, I will become emotionally bankrupt. It is a strange concept, but the reality is that if we pay the price correctly our emotional bank is restocked. People respond in a way that repays us for handling the cost correctly.

Again, this is a natural part of the process of grief, and we will have to pay the price. If we don't, if we try to avoid these events, we will suffer for it and become emotionally bankrupt and unable to respond correctly in each situation, and it will affect other areas of our life.

That reminder of our loss exacts a price emotionally. We are thrown back for a moment into our grief. The moment may be brief or could be long. Not important. It is the price you pay for losing your loved one. Don't be afraid to make this payment. It is healthy and an encouragement. Some might say that if there had been pain and problems in the relationship, it might not be healthy. But truthfully, whether the relationship was sound and incredible or difficult and fraught with struggle, if we make the payment in a healthy manner, in time, we will grow and benefit. It is a debt we pay to ourselves and those around us.

Does this make sense?

It is a bit like the importance of telling someone you love them. It is the cost of loving them. The more we pay, the greater the dividends and blessings that accrue. Telling someone you care about that they are important is a similar payment we make. Not because we are selfish and want something from them, but because it is the right thing to do. If we do so for the right reason, then it is healthy for both parties.

In the same way, paying this price is healthy. The key is paying in a healthy manner. And even as I say, a healthy manner, I am somewhat at a loss to clearly define what that means. Each person will need to discover what this is. Some may need to go into isolation for a limited time to process all that has happened. Others will need contact and interaction with others to work through all the issues. In all of the options, having key people who are walking with us through the process is critical. Not that we have to have programmed debriefing or regular conversations. But that we have people who represent safe ground and anchors that can be relied on when and if needed. They will help us see and understand what is happening and if we are dealing with the price of grief in a healthy manner.

But what about five, ten, or twenty years later? Do we keep paying a price for our grief? And now things get messy. Grief never fades to nothing. Grief is always present and marks us in some way. It leaves us with good memories, bad memories, happiness, and regrets. It may fade into the background but it never, as long as we are living, disappears. Some may think it is all behind them, and then, like a smell or sound that triggers a memory, it is back. This is because there is an innumerable list of possible items that can cause a flashback, a memory spike, or a reminder that my wife has died.

Do we keep paying a price? For some, the answer is a very clear yes. Each time a key event comes, they complete a ritual of remembrance. The most common is to go to the cemetery and place flowers on the grave site of the person who has died. How often this occurs will depend on the person. It could be at every key event in their relationship: engagement, marriage, birthday, and so on. This can last for years and even for the rest of their life. There is in us a need to honor and remember that person and to do so means paying a price, in time and resources. To not do so creates too many questions and conflicts about if we truly loved them.

For some, the action is very private and only a few close people know

that they are carrying out this ritual. For others, there are very public in-
dicators. Today, the most common would be a brief reminder on social
media that it has been so many years since the person died. Another would
be in the form of stating that it would have been their ___ nth birthday, our
___ nth anniversary, and so on. There is an internal need to be sure that people know we remember these events and so declare our love and concern.

   Why do we do this? I can think of a few reasons.

- We have an emotional need that can only be satisfied with such
  an action.
- There is a fear that others may not believe we truly loved that
  person if we don't do something.
- We, for some reason, feel we owe that person, that we have a debt
  to pay for all we received from them.
- There was love so deep that we cannot not do so. To forget would
  be unthinkable.
- We are afraid that others may not remember and our loved one
  may become lost in oblivion.

   I am sure there are more possibilities and many shades and variations
of these. The point is, there is a need to respond, and our grief exacts from
us a payment to maintain balance.

   The problem here is not in carrying out these actions, it is in what we
hope to gain by doing them. Healthy grief and remembrance are cathartic
and beneficial. In time, it helps us move forward in life and beyond the
need to remember, to the joy of remembering. It helps us be comfortable
with others not remembering and not being turned inside out when someone comments about your wife not being present, and so on.

   But if it is to satisfy the expectations of others, then we will be in trouble. We are now paying someone else's debt or need to remember. We are
allowing another person to control our grief, and it will become a prison in
which we are trapped instead of a beautiful park that we can visit and relax
as needed.

   In this time frame, we will be confronted by another layer of cost.
This will often involve some very personal and yet very public actions on
our part: the day I take off my wedding ring, the day I take down photos
of us, the day I think of maybe, possibly, dare I say it, remarrying. While
you might say no one will notice the missing ring, that is an error. You

will notice and be very conscious of this fact. Family members may notice and comment. And if you are a widower, and all the stories about widows looking for a husband are true, then there is a large segment of society who will take notice.

Taking down pictures, changing pictures. Some of this will be more challenging. How does one take down a picture of the grandkids with their grandmother so it can be updated? Do you keep them both, and should the new one include you in the picture (another layer of reminders of who is now missing)? Do you replace the family picture that has your wife in it with the one without her? Do you take down pictures of your wife and replace them? How long do you leave up those photos and souvenirs that represent your marriage and replace them with something else, whether of your life now, or neutral?

How do you handle all the memorabilia that represents your life with your wife? How you handle these will provide wonderful reminders of your life, for you and others, or monstrous barriers to moving forward and defining your life without your wife. It all depends on how you are doing at dealing with the price of grief.

Grief does this to us. It forces us to make decisions about so many aspects of our life. It is part of the price. To say you won't deal with it is ludicrous. By saying that, you have chosen how you will pay for the grief that is now part of your life, and you will pay. Bottling up and avoiding what is unpleasant may give you space to process what has happened for a while, but it becomes destructive if maintained for too long. At some point, the pain, sorrow, and loss must be expressed if balance and emotional health are to be restored.

And now we are years down the path of loss. By now, one of two decisions has been made. I will never remarry and will pay the price of being a widower and single. Or I have remarried and will pay the price of mixing my world, my family, and my marriage history with that of another person. In the one, I live for the memory of the one I lost. In the other, I have to learn how to blend past and present.

Both require payments. The one in knowing how to not exclude others, the other in how to include others. The one living with the present in the past, the other living with the past in the present. The first means knowing how to make my present fit with my past. The second means knowing what of the past fits and is appropriate in the present.

As I write this, I am realizing that grief will be with me until I die. My task is to benefit as much as possible from what has happened. Grief will always exact from me a cost. My task is to decide what I want to pay, how I want to pay, and how I will use what I have paid for. It is almost like there are two items on a shelf for sale: one is called good grief, the other is bad grief.

I have choices to make. Some are clear and easy; others are difficult and challenging. It is like life; every step we take comes at a cost. Every step can be taken in joy and anticipation or anger and frustration. Taking the next step is not an option; you will do so. And if you think you can just stand still, that doesn't work because life does not stand still, and it will move you forward.

Grief is like that. And each step has its cost.

# Caregiver Syndrome

There is a lot of information on the web and other places about caregivers. The main focus is on those who must care for aging parents or someone who has been incapacitated due to a severe injury or sickness. There is a lot of stress in being on call 24/7, and so on.

But this is not about that type of caregiving. It is about something that we promise to do as a husband and wife and what is expected of us as parents.

When we get married, we make a promise to love, care for, and cherish our partner. Then we are given the conditions under which we are to carry out this promise. You know them well, in sickness and health, for richer or poorer, and until death brings an end to that relationship.

But what does all of that mean? And how do we provide the love, care, and cherishing that is involved?

Just so there is no confusion, let me try to explain it.

In a marriage, each partner brings certain skills and abilities to that marriage. Each is expected to use those abilities in carrying for each other. The areas usually involved are housekeeping, food preparation, laundry, home maintenance, and finances. These are the basics. There are others that can be included, but this will be sufficient.

There was a time when some of these were defined by gender. That was too bad because doing that could easily put the wrong person in charge of the wrong area. More and more now, the roles are not being defined solely by gender but also by ability, interest, and time available. Now there are stay-at-home dads and situations where both partners are employed. In both cases, who does what is altered, and at times, both take on a key responsibility on a rotation basis.

All that aside, there remains the fact that these are functions that define a caregiver: a person who provides for the needs of another person. And in marriage, this is definitely a 24/7 responsibility. There are no vacations in the sense that you can take time off and so force your partner to do everything. Well, to be honest, there are times when it can become the responsibility of one, when one of the people becomes ill and cannot fulfill their responsibility of a caregiver. This usually balances out over time as both individuals will get sick at different times.

And there will be times when both help each other out in key areas. When there is a large amount of lawn work, preparing for guests to come, the spring-cleaning thing, and so on. The point is that these two people have become the caregiver for each other. And this caregiving is 24/7 for the rest of their marriage. At least that is what they promised.

If they have children, then another layer of caregiving is added. Again, the normal way this works is for each to share in the responsibilities of feeding, bathing, cleaning, disciplining, teaching, and on the list goes. This will continue until . . . some would say until they move out and become independent. The truth is, while the level of care may diminish, the reality of caring for one's children never ends.

And when the grandchildren come, you will find yourself drawn into another type of caregiving. Usually, this one is fun because you don't have to provide care 24/7 but only for short periods of time. You get to enjoy them and then give them back.

During this time, you find yourself regressing back to how life was before there were children. You are now older and wiser, it is hoped. You may have shifted who does what over the years. It doesn't matter, you are still a 24/7 caregiver to your spouse. And by now you should also be the one providing support for special activities and interests. My wife had a puppet ministry, and I built at least three puppet stages over the years. She had an interest in providing care for children with AIDS, and so I helped build a home for those children. I began writing, and she became my editor in chief. We cared for each other's interests and activities.

In all of this, the hope is that all will go well, and you will live a long life together being each other's caregiver. The person who is there 24/7 to provide emotional help, be there to encourage each other's spiritual growth and relationship with God, to enjoy their gifts and talents, and do whatever is needed to make life a blessing, because you are there and share in all that is happening together.

That is what we hope. But there are so many things that can challenge the balanced caregiving we hope and strive for. We all know what can happen: accidents, changes in economics, serious health concerns, and other items. And those are just related to our marriage. There can be outside events that affect us and those around us that will flip our world over, tornadoes, fires, floods, and hurricanes. They may not affect us directly but can affect family and friends, which may alter our plans. And finally, our families are not immune to events that can alter the lives of children, parents, and others that we are close to, resulting in us needing to enter a new level of caregiving that can strain our caregiving for each other.

The most challenging one is when your spouse dies. In that moment, all that 24/7 caregiving is gone. You often do not realize how this will impact you at first. If you are part of a caring community, there will be people who will offer to help you with many things. They may cook meals, help with maintenance, and so. The help will often reflect who died, the husband or the wife.

But in time, whoever is left behind will have to take over all of the caregiving responsibilities. They may not actually do them all, but they are now responsible for all that was once shared between two people. There are what looks like three stages in this process. There is the first stage where people provide help in key areas as needed. The second stage is where you learn to take over all those responsibilities. The third stage is when you hit the wall. All that caregiving overwhelms you. Not that you are not capable of doing everything. You have learned to adapt your schedule to allow the time and energy needed to make it work.

What happens is that you hit an emotional wall, and the reality that your partner in caregiving is gone. You are having to do it all alone. And it doesn't matter if you can call on others to help as needed, you are still the one making all the decisions and organizing what needs to be done. And there is no one there to talk to about what to do and when.

There is no one to help with cleaning the house, cooking the meals, doing the laundry, going with you to see the kids and grandkids. You are alone as you travel. And the silence can be overwhelming. You have no one to talk to about what is happening and help with the planning. No second opinions and discussion. Yes, you may say you have family and friends. But be honest, it is not the same. They are not available 24/7 like your spouse was.

Your emotions will go up and down as you deal with this each day. There will be high times and then low times. The low times will be caused by the reality that your spouse is not there to enjoy special days and activities, which you now must do alone. The high times are when you feel good about life and people are actively engaged in your world. But again, it can't be the same. Your caregiver partner is gone, and there is no replacement, at least for the foreseeable future. This reality may be a cause for some to remarry as soon as possible. Having to live without a caregiver is a frightening concept, especially if you have been married for a significant time. Or, if you are doing double duty, mom and dad, for your children. But that is another topic, and my focus here is what I am experiencing with the loss of my caregiver.

This reality has become even more focused for me over the last year. It is the sickness and health part. Both of us cared for each other when sick. We both have had to deal with some serious short-term health issues. And for twelve years, we dealt with being each other's caregiver when my wife was diagnosed with stage four cancer. It shifted some of the caregiving responsibility depending on how the chemo was affecting her. But it never rendered her completely incapable of providing for my care in some way. If she couldn't help me with the physical things, she always was capable of caring for me emotionally and spiritually.

But now that is gone.

I have dealt with two minor health issues over the past eighteen months. Nothing serious enough to require hospitalization, and yet sufficiently long in their impact as to affect my life and my activity during this past eighteen months. Partly because I have had to have three outpatient procedures, each of which has required time for the recovery process. This fact, and how to deal with recovery, has highlighted the fact that I have no caregiver. Thankfully, friends have stepped to take me to the hospital and, on occasion, spend a night to be sure all was well. But there is no one who can be here 24/7.

I sometimes think my kids should be more involved. They should call me more. They should do this or do that. But that is unrealistic and unfair. I have not been that sick. What I have been is alone, and that aloneness has highlighted how much I depended on my wife as my caregiver 24/7.

It highlights the reality that my helper, my caregiver in so many areas of my life, is gone. It highlights the fact that while I can call on people to care for very specific needs – rides to the airport, sharing a meal, and a few other areas – I don't have access to any one person at the level of the caregiver that I have lost.

I call this the caregiver syndrome because it has multiple elements.

1.  The daily needs of caring for cooking, cleaning, laundry, and shopping for what is needed.
2.  The emotional support that has been lost. It can be provided by others but not at the same level and context.
3.  The spiritual support since I don't have one who is praying and sharing with me at this level. Again, others can pray and encourage, but they cannot live with me and see exactly what is happening.

4. Financial decisions that must be made. Others can be consulted, but they will not live with the results like I have to. When you have a 24/7 caregiver, it affects how you process these decisions because you consider how it affects both of you.

5. Health issues are a challenging one. You both had a person available around the clock, someone you could wake up in the middle of the night, someone who was at your side. The only way you get that kind of care is in a hospital or a nursing home. That lack of a person can have quite an impact, less if you have no serious or only semi-serious issues. But if they are such that they create stress about what could happen because you are alone or who could you call if you really need someone, then it becomes an issue.

A syndrome exists because multiple things accumulate to create an environment where stress and worry can begin to affect you mentally and physically. This is more likely if you are not paying attention to what is happening and have no one to talk to about your caregiver needs.

Each of the above areas has its way of impacting you and how well you handle the changes. The problem or syndrome is when too many of them are happening at the same time and the intensity of what is happening increases. If all is going well, then you can handle it all, but let one of these areas become complicated and too intense, and you can get lost in your grief.

Grief and loss will take us down this path. The key to managing what will happen and the changes that will occur is becoming aware of these issues and having a support group to talk to that provides encouragement and guidance as you navigate all the changes that occur because you no longer have a caregiver, your spouse. That way, if an area begins to approach being difficult to manage, you will have people to go to for help and encouragement, and that will help you keep your balance, thus providing needed stability to properly handle what may be happening.

# Excess Baggage or Ticket to Tomorrow

At some point, all the past will become excess baggage or a ticket into the future. To explain this, I will use two other terms that I recently heard used to explain a key point of decision for that person. They used the phrases *moving on* and *moving forward*.

*Moving on* — this phrase suggests that there is a past that must be left behind. It implies that a person needs to shed some kind of burden in order to move forward, to rid themselves of the excess baggage they have accumulated and are trying to bring with them. The image is of the person who packs every conceivable thing they might need, stress the phrase *might need*, for a trip, instead of thinking of taking only what is absolutely necessary and so, as one would say, travel light.

A common phrase used in this context is *emotional baggage*: all the feelings that bind us to an event, relationship, or location. The image is of things that slow us down or drag a person down so they cannot advance and even may become stalled where they are.

The most common result of this overloading or burden is depression, the inability to manage the emotions and challenges that are part of what has happened in their life. It can be caused by the feeling that one cannot overcome what has happened or cannot deal with all that has happened as a result of events (serious illness), poor decisions (impact of alcoholism), or the actions of others, which pressure the person or trap them in destructive relations.

This is too much to cover, and since the focus is on grief, then the key area of concern is the impact of the death of a loved one, in my case my spouse. Even in this event, the range of impact is great. For some, it can be mild. They have a strong wellness system and network of friends. For others, it can be severe because of the level of dependence on the relationship. But hear this very clearly, there is no guarantee that either of these people will manage the loss well or be buried by it.

A person with a strong system of support can just as easily become lost in the emotions and struggles as one who doesn't, and people who have little support can surprise us with their resilience. Strong or weak, the issues don't change. We have entered a way of living that involves a great loss, and we are now dealing with the grief that is part of that loss, whether we want to or not.

Grief is real and impacts a person at so many levels: emotional, physical, spiritual, and relational. And the evidence of this truth is that it is never far from our thoughts and is always reminding us of what has happened. This can be so intense that people need to become part of a special support group. I have talked with a friend of mine whose husband died fourteen years ago, and she saw the need for such a group to help others deal with their grief. They meet weekly to help manage the loss and the grief that comes with the death of a spouse.

I find it interesting that the groups that specialize in helping people deal with the baggage in their lives, the past failures, bad decisions, and the like, do not tell people to move on. What they tell them is to face what has happened, find help and strength in others, and learn how to use what has happened to become a better person. If you enter a group session of AA and you are asked to share, you begin with your name and the declaration that you are an alcoholic. And it doesn't matter how many years of sobriety you may have accumulated you still begin with this declaration, "I am an alcoholic (or drug addict)," and so on.

I have noted also that people who deal with different emotional challenges, like depression, bipolar disorder, and others are quite offended by those who try to minimize what is happening by saying they should get over it and move on. It just doesn't work like that. For some, there are medicines to help them to manage the severity of what is happening, but they still need to identify the truth of their situation and learn to manage what is happening. This is best done in the context of people who are willing to learn about what is happening and be supportive in the process of managing the impact of what has happened and how it will continue to impact their lives.

So, moving on is not an option. You cannot sever yourself from the past. You may be able to lessen its impact, but you cannot move on and leave it behind as if it were a piece of furniture. You know you are moving, and there is no room in the vehicle for one more item or no room in the place where you are going for that item. But if you think about it, you really don't leave it behind. The memory of the item and the decision to not take it with remains with you.

This is how grief is. You make decisions about giving away your spouse's clothing, jewelry, books, and other items. Often to children, family, and friends. At least the things they may want. You decide what must be given away, the items no one can use, and what you can't use. I gave a lot of my wife's clothing to the church for a fundraiser. But you can't give away the memories of those items, and I am not talking about remembering every specific item, but the fact that you have given them away or disposed of them. That remains with you because they were part of your life, they appear in pictures, but now people you know have them, and so on.

You cannot remove the memories. You can't just move on because that all remains with you, no matter how much you may try to forget or ignore it. You may have reduced the physical baggage, but you really cannot remove the emotional baggage that will remain. You really can't move on, can't separate yourself from the past. Trying to do this is not healthy. But you can move forward.

*Moving forward* — this was the phrase the caught my attention. All that stuff will remain with you in one form or another. Some of it in the form of memories, history, pictures. A large part of it because it is who you are. All of that baggage – that history, your life up until the moment your spouse died – and grief entered your life, came together to make you the person you are.

While some may think that discarding this item and selling that item may suggest you are moving on and leaving the past behind, that is a misconception. Discarding and removing the objects doesn't change what they meant and how they were part of what you have become. Taking down the pictures, packing away sentimental objects, may remove them from sight and suggest that you are moving on, but that is not true. They may no longer be visible to others, but anyone who knows you will see and realize they are part of who you have become. Denying this is foolish and potentially harmful.

I have much to learn about this process. It has been less than two years since my wife died. I am a bit afraid of how to handle the truth that no matter what I do, my wife and all our life together will always be with me. There is no moving on. You don't discard that. But how does one manage this as they move forward to encounter new people and new experiences?

Being with old friends and in familiar places does not require as much. They know the story, for they have been part of it. They become concerned when there is no evidence of moving forward when life is only lived in the past, and the past does not help us live in the present.

What scares me is how this will work as I meet new people. How will all that I am now allow me to move forward and be a part of another person's world and life? The person who suggested these two concepts shared this. Summary of her presentation: The person I met realized that who I am today is because of all that I gained from my past, including my prior marriage (my husband died of cancer). At the same time, I had to realize that all the other person is was the result of their past life and relationships (a similar event to mine). When we realized that we could benefit from each other's history and stories and create a new and beneficial one in the present and for the future, we moved forward. (TEDWomen 2018 Podcast – Nora McInerny.)

Managing grief correctly will help us understand the difference between treating our past as excess baggage or a ticket to the future, a blessing that can be used and be a benefit to any relationships we may develop in the years to come.

As the AA introduction goes, "Hello, my name is Perry and I am a widower." That is who I am. I can choose to try and cut myself free from the past, excess baggage, and move on, not recommended; or I can choose to embrace all of that and treat it as a ticket to move forward.

My Poems About Grief

# Uneven Ground

There has been an earthquake
It opened a chasm and it cannot be crossed
There has been an earthquake
It has broken the ground and it cannot be crossed
There has been an earthquake
It has displaced the world and it cannot be restored
There has been an earthquake
It has blocked the way and it cannot be reopened
There has been an earthquake
It has separated us but we will be reunited
There has been an earthquake
It has broken our hearts but we will find life
There has been an earthquake
It has fractured our emotions but we will find wholeness
There has been an earthquake
It has clouded our thoughts but not forever
There has been an earthquake
It has caused pain but one day all pain will end

The earthquake separated you from me
    But it could not take you out of my life
The earthquake created changes in my life
    But it could not change my love for you
The earthquake devastated my world
    But it could not destroy your blessing
The earthquake restructured my activities
    But could not alter all that you mean to me.
I love you and miss you so much. So grateful for all the memories of
    our life together that give strength to each day and everything I do.
Your loving husband

# Grief — A Strange Emotion

Grief is a strange emotion
In one moment, it crushes with the loss
No more hugs
No more sharing
In another moment, it lifts you in joy
A memory in a photo
A shared experience
Grief is a strange emotion
In one moment, it brings you to your knees
In the pain of the loss
In the pain of the loneliness
In another moment, it makes you soar
As you realize the gift given
As you realize they are alive in heaven
Grief is a strange emotion
In one moment, it creates total loss of control
Bringing tears and sobs to rack you
Bringing soul-wrenching pain
In another moment, it focuses your vision
Restoring your humanity
Restoring your faith
Grief is a strange emotion
In a moment, it renders you comatose
Making you numb and senseless
Making you lost and homeless
In another moment, it restores your perspective
Deepening your capacity to love
Deepening your capacity to share life
Grief is a strange emotion
In one moment, it robs you of your self-control
Muddling your thinking
Confusing your direction
In another moment, it teaches you to grow
Guiding you into new opportunities
Providing doors, you never saw before
Grief is a strange emotion

In one moment, it slams a door in your face
   Denying access to what is gone
   Making you uncertain of what comes next
In another moment, it opens new paths
   Relationships with others
   Deeper knowledge of God
Grief, true grief, is honored by God
 While it strips away our façade – a necessary thing
 While it quietly brings us to truth – our heavenly Father

# I Want to Be Angry

I want to be angry
    It is my right to be angry
They took her away without my permission
I need to be angry
    It is my right to be angry
There is so much hurt and pain inside
I wish to be angry
    It is my right to be angry
And I stop and wonder why I have this need
    And so, I pause and reflect
She died, but we knew that day would come
    Death is a part of life
        It can come in a moment
            A truck crushes out life
        It can come over time
            Age exacts its payment
    Death is a promised result
        It reminds us of our sinful state
            We are doomed to die
        It reminds us of what must be done
            Victory over death is possible
She died and we knew the cause
    Death will always have a cause
        Will we blame God
            For not healing
        Will we blame others
            For any reason possible
        Will we blame ourselves
            Because of what we should have . . .
    Death clearly has a cause
        It is the result of sin
            No one can escape this
        It is a haunting reality
            Until we understand
        It is a challenge to us
            To learn the truth

She died and all our plans and hopes ended
    Death changes the course of life
        It ends a relationship
            The physical contact
        It ends all future plans
            With that person
    Death reorients our world
        It opens us to new paths
            To new relationships
        It opens us to new challenges
            A source of new hope and direction
I want to be angry
    It is my right to be angry
A lie that can destroy us
I need to be angry
    It is my right to be angry
A futile action that will change nothing
I wish I could be angry
    It is my right to be angry
Let the pain pass so joy can come

# Space — Too Many Spaces

Spaces too many spaces
    One by one they reveal what has been lost
    One by one they expose the pain and hurt
    One by one they threaten to undo me
Spaces – Where we sat and held each other
    Talking about life
    Talking about family
    Talking about causes
Spaces – Where we sat and hugged
    Letting silence speak to us of love
    Letting silence give God access
    Letting silence remind us of blessings
Spaces – Where we lay and cuddled
    Resting in each other's love
    Resting in a time to restore strength
    Resting to encourage each other
Spaces – Where we worked and dreamed
    Struggling to organize our ministry
    Struggling to encourage each other
    Struggling to understand those we served
Spaces – Where we chatted and connected
    Establishing bonds with each other
    Establishing channels of communication
    Establishing doors for others to enter
Spaces – Where we cried and learned to trust
    Knowing God understood our pain
    Knowing God had a plan to prosper us
    Knowing God was not surprised by tears
Spaces – Where we question and grew in love
    Hearing God speak quietly of love
    Hearing God show how to help each other
    Hearing God reveal what he was doing
Spaces – Where I now sit, stand, and walk alone
    Wishing for her presence and touch
    Wishing for her words and encouragement
    Wishing for her hugs and her smile

Spaces – Where I now sit, stand, and walk in anticipation
  Waiting for God to ease the pain
  Waiting for God to fill the void
  Waiting for God to teach me more
Spaces too many spaces
  One by one they reveal themselves
  One by one God uses to prepare me
  One by one they teach me His love

# On the Edge

I stand on a precipice
Looking down
I see a nothing
    A pit
     Without bottom
    A pit
     Filled with blackness
    A pit
     That I must cross
I stand on a precipice
 Looking out
  I see my goal
   A destination
    Without crossing
   A destination
    Filled with options
   A destination
    That I must reach
I stand on a precipice
 Looking on
  I want to know
   The step
    Which I must take
   The step
    Which will give access
   The step
    That will not cause pain
I stand on a precipice
 Looking in
  I see danger
   The fear
    Which blocks me
   The fear
    Fills my awareness
   The fear
    That hinders my choice

I stand on a precipice
  Looking around
    I want to see
     My love
    Who gave me strength
     My love
    Who lifted my heart
     My love
    Who was with me
I stand on a precipice
  Looking for sight
    Knowing what to do
     I step
    Believing God will
     I step
    To learn what will be
     I step
    And remember life
I stand on a precipice
  Looking up
    I have to see
     The path
    I have to walk
     The path
    I have the goal
     The path
    Not seen until
I step
    It is not a precipice

Today would have been Nancy's sixty-first birthday. As I have looked through our photos and thinking about my wife, I am even more convinced that she was more beautiful than the day I met her. To capture why I believe this and my love for her I have written the following note and poem and prepared a video.

Nancy, on this your birthday I offer the following:

As the day approached and I looked through the photos I have taken of my amazing wife I saw the evidence of something I have seen and believe to be true: My wife had become more beautiful over the years, and I knew why. She loved God more than me, and that made her love for me perfect in every way.

I miss her greatly. I miss seeing her smile, watching her beauty shine and touch my life and the lives of others.

## Nancy — A Woman of Eternal Beauty

I am a proud man
    Better I am a blessed man
Proud because you were my wife
    Blessed because of your inner beauty
You were beautiful the day I met you
    Your beauty captured my eyes
    And then your inner beauty
        That smile
            Captured my heart

That beauty lit up your face and kept you forever young
    Each stage of life deepened your beauty
        Each child a new avenue to demonstrate your beauty
    Each ministry allowed more to enjoy and learn
        The source of your beauty
    Each challenge faced revealed its power and its source
The words from your Lord focused it
        Allowed you to have a willing spirit
        Allowed to know and follow God's plan

Allowed you to be a channel of God's blessing
Even the worst news of all, Cancer, could not dim your beauty
It tried to rob you of your dignity
It tried to distort your appearance
It tried to rob you of focus and energy
It tried to distort your spirit
In every intent to ruin your beauty
It only shone brighter and more evident
And all could see its power through that smile
The smile that captured my heart that first day

I am a proud man
Better I am a blessed man
Proud because you are my wife
Blessed because your beauty has filled my world.

I am a proud man
Better I am a blessed man
Proud because I had the most beautiful woman at my side
Blessed because God was at the center of your beauty

# The Tides of Grief

It's alive
 It keeps on coming
   Like a tide, it flows
     Over me
     Around me
     Through me
It's alive
 It won't go away
   Like the rhythm of the tide
     Repeating itself
     Renewing its presence
     Restoring its place
It's alive
 It wants to crush me
   Like a rogue, it flows
     Unstoppable
     Unrelenting
     Unrepeating
It's alive
 It builds and builds
   Like a tsunami
     Gathering its force
     Preparing to arise
     Erupting in fury
It's alive
 It repeats itself every day
   With highs and lows
     Rising up one moment
     Waning away the next
     Always in motion
It's alive
 And will never go away
   It has become my new rhythm
     Cycling my life
     Rebuilding my reality
     Reshaping how I live.

# The Question Always Asked

It was asked
 I became uncertain
It was asked
 They became sheepish
It was asked
 I dodged the answer
It was asked
 They sighed in relief

It was asked
 It brought up pain
It was asked
 It left them wondering
It was asked
 It carried me away
It was asked
 It shut them out

It was asked
 They wanted to know more
It was asked
 I wanted to be understood
It was asked
 They could not go forward
It was asked
 I could not let them enter

It was asked
 It created an awkward moment
It was asked
 It revealed the chasm between
It was asked
 It brought no connection
It was asked
 It created no help

It was asked

The person smiled in uncertainty
It was asked
   I strained to find a way to share
It was asked
   The person could not wait
It was asked
   I remained in my world alone

# I Regret

I regret
>But you will never know

I regret
>But you never judged me

I regret
>But it will not change the blessing

I wish
>I had said and done more

I wish
>I had hugged and cuddled more

I wish
>I had one more chance to be more

I regret
>And then am thankful for what we had

I regret
>And then our love frees me from the trap

I regret
>And then what we had restores my future

I wish
>To choose, to let regret fade into truth

I wish
>To remember, to enjoy the wonder of our life

I wish
>To rejoice, to honor the blessing that is now

# Alone Lonely

I hear no activity
   I see no shadows
      I feel no presence
      But
What does that mean
   What does that reveal
      What does that imply
Am I alone or lonely?
I hear no interaction
   I see no movement
      I feel no contact
      But
Is it possible to identify?
   Is it possible to perceive?
      Is it possible to exist?
Am I alone or lonely?
I hear no response
   I see no effect
      I feel no reality
      But

Does that mean oblivious
   Does that mean isolation
      Does that mean emptiness
Am I alone or lonely?
I hear no reply
   I see no logic
      I feel no effect
      But
What does that suggest
   What does this disclose
      What does this involve
Am I alone or lonely?
I hear nothing that is different
   I see nothing that survives
      I feel nothing that refreshes

But
What do I want to hear?
What do I want to see?
What do I want to feel?
Am I alone or lonely?
In the answers, I will know
And then learn
When alone becomes lonely
When lonely is just being alone
Am I alone or lonely?
In the answers, I will know
And then learn
When I need to be alone
When being lonely is good
Am I alone or lonely?
In the answers, I will know
And then learn
How to not be alone
How to face lonely
Am I alone or lonely?
In the answers, I will know
And then learn
I will have to learn to wait
I will be free to be
Alone but not lonely

# Silence Reigns

I have entered a dead calm
  No sound can be heard
    I can't see
A vacuum has drawn out all air
  No sound can be made
    I can't see
A deafening roar has begun
  All sound is extinguished
    I can't see
The dead calm prevents movement
  I can find no way to hear
    I can't see
The vacuum creates a loss of control
  A sound made can't be heard
    I can't see
The deafening road dominates my existence
  If a sound is made, what then?
    I can't see
The dead calm means no advance is possible
  Speaking gains nothing
    I can't see
The vacuum exposes emptiness
  Speaking can affect nothing
    I can't see
The deafening roar means my emotions rule
  Speaking is but useless
    I can't see
But then I see
The dead calm can be controlled by peace
  There is another voice
    Seeing is not necessary
The vacuum can be infused beyond what is known
  There is hope, love, and faith
    Seeing is not necessary
The deafening road can be muzzled
  There is one who can create quiet
    Seeing is not necessary

# Renewal

I mourn again
    I cry
                I weep
    I die
I grieve again
    I ache
                I moan
    I quake
I breathe again
    I glance
                I move
    I dance

# The Pendulum

The pendulum swings
    It takes me away
        It brings me back
It has a rhythm
    It has a stroke
        A path it follows
    A high point – no two
        A low point – just one
It has a power
    It has a force
        A path it creates
    A place light – no two
        A place hard – just one
It has a cycle
    It has a constant
        A path it repeats
    A place free – no two
        A place bound – just one
The pendulum swings
    It takes me away
        It brings me back
It is memory
    It has a screen
        A place to review
    A place quiet – no two
        A place strident – just one
It is a person
    It has a focus
        A purpose it serves
    A place to renew – no two
        A place to cry – just one
It is a tempo
    It has an effect
        A purpose to create
    A place to live – no two
        A place to strain – just one

You are the pendulum
    You bring me joy
            You bring me sorrow
    Twice the joy as you swing
            With every stroke of sorrow
You are the pendulum
    Slowly swinging in and out
            But ever present
    Reminding me
            Of all you were
You are the pendulum
    Swinging away to allow for the new
    Swinging back to give me strength
You are the pendulum
    Keeping the rhythm
    Defining the path
    Moving me forward

At this time of year, I am reminded of the wonder and beauty of my wife. It is like a pendulum swinging back that brings with it all the wonderful memories that provide the ability to continue doing all the ministry God called us to do. Nancy may be gone in a physical sense, but over and over I am able to enjoy the blessing of her presence in my life. Most recently as people came to speak to me and reminisce about the times we had been together with them. These days, as a friend of ours is here and sharing in ministry with me, and in the days ahead as her birthday, our anniversary, and Christmas come, it is a wonderful time to enjoy again the incredible gift that I was given when he brought Nancy into my life and allowed us to serve together. And while this can be a challenging time, days like birthdays and anniversaries do bring a level of sorrow and reminders of the fact that she is no longer with me and we can no longer celebrate them together. They also bring reminders of all the blessings that we had together through the years that God gave us.

May God do the same for each of you. May he bring people into your life that bring joy and more as you serve in the kingdom of God.

# Well Digging

Into the depths
 The well we dig
 A fountain tapped
 A uniting focus
Begin the task
 Create the resource
 Deeper by the day
 A testing of vows
Clear the earth
 Seek the table
 One to dig
 One to lift
Finding the source
 Going deeper still
 Dig for the future
 Provide for change
Into the depths
 The well of life
 A fountain tapped
 A guiding vision
Protect the work
 Shore up the well
 Increases the hope
 Proves the goal
Secure the past
 Make the work last
 Begin the giving
 Drawing for others
Exist in its hope
 made accessible
 bounty for all
 strength to grow
Into the depths
 The well of giving
 A foundation tapped
 A living heritage

Providing life
  Beyond the loss
  In the grief
  Creator of hope
Drawing others in
  The depth is proved
  The hope renews
  Others joined in living
Creating a pattern
  What life can become
  What focus generates
  A well revitalized
Into the depths
  The well we dug
  A foundation tapped
  An enduring work of love

# Moving On, Moving Forward

Moving on
    Such a destructive concept
    To forget all I have done
            Should I cut off a hand?
    To forget everywhere I have been
            Should I cut off a foot?
    To forget everything I have observed
            Should I gouge out an eye?
    To eliminate all I have gained
            Do I remove half of my brain?
    To leave behind what is lost
            Is it possible to excise emotion?

Moving forward
    Such a constructive concept
    To use all I have done
            to create a foundation for what lies ahead
    to use all I have encountered
            to establish a clear direction to my path
    to use all I have observed
            to be a canvas to create a grander mural
    to use all I have gained
            to form a framework for more growth
    to use all of my history
            to give renewed life to my emotion

# Reflections

This collection of materials is about the emotions and issues that I have encountered in the journey of grief. They are based on my attempt to identify what was happening as well as the comments of others that opened my thinking to other aspects of what I was going through.

I have been reflecting on all that has happened and what I am learning about myself, what Nancy meant to me, and what happens when one loses their life partner. I would like to share with you what I am learning about loss and God's presence.

# Booby Traps, Landmines, Time Bombs, and the Nuke

These last three months since my wife, Nancy, died have been filled with a variety of emotional challenges and experiences. The title represents aspects of what has been happening in my life. Let me explain further.

**The nuke** – This is what happens in the moment of a loved one's passing. There is a huge emotional explosion that occurs. It is what happens the moment you realize that your wife has died and is forever gone. Any attempt to restrain this or try to delay, cover up, or evade it is usually futile and can be harmful. Bottling this up only can cause greater damage, like an atomic bomb. The emotions must be released in a controlled manner to survive the devastating effect of the loss.

But after the explosion, there is the fallout. Like a nuclear explosion, often the greatest impact is not in the initial event but in the fallout that will follow. The events that will be affected because of the loss. I am in the midst of the fallout. I am experiencing events by myself that were planned with both of us in mind. These events cannot be canceled because that doesn't allow for the proper release of the emotions and a chance to heal from the impact of that event. They are activities and trips that were made with both of us in mind that I have had to carry out alone or with someone other than my wife. The effects are both subtle and openly noticed in what you are doing and how you communicate with those around you. You begin to deal with the "I" instead of the "we" and it causes a deep ache in the soul.

I wish I could tell you how long this goes on for, but I can't. Each relationship is different, and what was planned will be different. I only know that there is fallout, and the best way to handle it is by sharing it with people with whom you are close and who know what is going on. It helps to have someone who knows how the healing process varies and who can also see when the sharing is bringing healing or simply reopening the wounds and therefore preventing you from healing. It is a delicate issue and requires an openness and sensitivity that must be developed and can only be developed in the process of sharing what is happening.

**The time bomb** – This is different from the nuke, or the initial explosion. This is about repetition. We go through everyday motions. Things we have always done: Walk the same path, play the same music, cook, eat, and so on. What happens is that the accumulation of exposure to something reaches a tipping point, and the emotions break out.

I love cooking. I am a fairly good cook. I often had to cook for both of us when the effects of chemo were too much for Nancy to do so. And so, every day I cook and then I smell something I have smelled for weeks or do something I have been doing for weeks, and then one of those times I am frozen by the reality of what has been missing and the aloneness that it reveals.

I walk into the bedroom all the time. Then one time I realize that before when I entered that door, Nancy was always there. Or I look at my office door every day, and then one day I can't look at the door because I know that she will never walk through that door again to ask me a question, to call me to dinner, to just talk, and so on.

These are the paths that memory has worn into my life, my thinking, and how we lived, and they are still there as a reminder of what is missing. In time, they will fade, dim, and disappear, or be replaced by the new reality. But it takes time, and you never know when it will catch you unaware and remind you.

I sometimes wonder if it is even possible for these paths to ever fully fade. I sometimes wonder and then realize they should stay because they led us to others who became part of those journeys and need me to continue to walk them.

**Land mines** – these represent activities of life that were not part of our everyday life. They lie in wait around the corners and amidst the seemingly normal. They were part of life and usually represent something important or special but are not life events like birthdays and anniversaries. Those we expect to bring sad memories and are part of the fallout above. I encounter land mines in the places we liked to go, the activities we enjoyed, and people we liked to spend time with. They happened sporadically or maybe on a somewhat regular basis, but not daily or even weekly.

You don't even think about them, and then one day you find yourself in that place, doing that activity, talking to that friend, and going to that restaurant, and she is not there with you or waiting for you. They are unpredictable, and you can't avoid them until you are face to face with that activity, place, or person. Then, you realize just how important and special it was. At the moment, it may have seemed normal or regular; but now, you realize how much that place or person fed your love and marriage.

**Booby traps** – These are things that are just hiding and waiting to blow up. You don't know where they are or what item, event, place, conversation, or any number of a hundred things may cause you to go all blurry-eyed and even choke up and cry. You open a door, and there is her special mug. You open a photo file, and there is a photo that brings out the emotions. You see a piece of clothing you donated to the church garage sale on another lady. Someone comes up to you and makes a comment, and you can't see straight or respond with any sense of control in your voice.

They didn't mean for that to happen, but it does, and you wonder what else may lay in wait. You can become paranoid and start avoiding places and people, and anything you think might cause an uncontrollable reaction. The reality is that booby traps don't allow for you to hide. The truth is, you are one who is setting the traps. It is your memories and loss that create the paths and activities where they will be hiding. And it is your memory that sets them off. So, unless you can do an erase and complete a reboot of your brain, then you cannot avoid them.

In fact, none of the above can be avoided unless you go into complete seclusion. But even that would not be enough. You would need to completely avoid any memory of the past, and that is a dangerous thing to do. It will not only seriously damage your ability to function but will harm all those who knew and loved your spouse.

So, there you have it. This is what I am learning to deal with since my wife died. It is scary at times, and yet at others, it is a great comfort. It is scary because they all remind me of the fact she is gone, and I no longer can enjoy her at my side. But it is a great comfort because of all that I gained having her as MY WIFE for thirty-eight years.

As you probably have noted, I have not shared any special scriptures or any incredible insights from the Bible. Yet, in fact, I have. One cannot share like this if they don't have a fall-back plan or safe place to go to. I have that, not because I have read a special scripture, despite the abundance of scriptures dealing with grieving (just look at all the cards that have been designed to comfort those who are grieving). I have a safe place because of the relationship I have with the One who gave us all of those words of comfort.

To be honest, without that relationship, those words found in scripture have no power to carry one through the pain and sorrow of the loss. They have no power to fill the gap that is created. They have no power to heal the wounds caused by the loss. They have no power to give strength in facing all the above. But, if you have a relationship with the source of those words, then you will understand that God is the pasture; he is the still water; he is our protector in dark places and our provider when we feel we have lost everything. He is, and that is enough.

I guarantee there will be a nuke and fallout. I guarantee there will be time bombs, landmines, and booby traps, and you must learn to navigate through the impact of such a loss. And I can guarantee that God, the one who brought us together, the one who decided it was time for her to go home and be healed, the one who gave me an incredible gift, will be there to lift and lead in all that lies ahead.

I am on the journey. I don't know where it will take me, but I know the Lord is with me.

# Tide, Rogue Wave, Tsunami — the Waves of Grief

As I continue on my journey in grief, I am becoming aware of more aspects of grief. At first, I was painfully aware of the things that I will call the shock aspects of grief. Now, I am learning that there is another aspect of grief that is repetitive in nature. As a result, I am discovering that grief is an incredibly complex emotion and is impacted by many circumstances and environmental factors. I base some of this reality on what I am experiencing and observations of how others are still grieving, even after many years have passed since the event.

To some extent, this perplexed me. Why do these people ten, twenty, thirty years, and more have a need to express their loss and their grief to others? Why do they decide that they need to do something for everyone on a global scale and not personally? A song for everyone, a scripture for everyone, or a poem for everyone who may need encouragement today based on their experience of grief and need for the same in their life.

At first, I thought there must be some deeper emotional or psychological issues, something that was still unresolved after so many years. As a result, there is still a need to deal with this past issue by paying forward into the lives of others. That works for some of the settings and people, but not all of them. For some, there is no hidden agenda or buried emotional struggle that is allowed out, a chance to release pent-up energy and prevent emotional collapse.

At first, I didn't understand, but now I am beginning to see a little of what may be going on, and beginning to understand that grief is not a single event but an ongoing experience that is now a permanent part of my life. I will never escape its presence and impact on me, my life, and those I interact with. This is most evident in the question, "How are you doing?" That used to be a pretty standard question with a very normal purpose, to learn how life, in general, was progressing.

Now it has changed. The old content and intent are still there, wanting to know how our life, in general, is. Now there is another aspect. It now includes, "How are you doing since . . . ?" It is not spoken that way, but it is there, as part of the question. And I don't foresee any change in this altered content for a long time to come.

And I am becoming aware that I am asking the same question of myself, how am I doing since my wife died? Not exactly in those words, but with that focus. And as I became aware of this, I also became troubled by the possibility that this question might not go away, that somehow my grief would be a permanent part of who I am and how my life will be lived from now on.

This caused me to think about what I was experiencing and what I was seeing in the lives of others and their expressions of grief. That reflection led me to the ideas in the title, natural events that are part of the ongoing reality of our life on this planet that helped me gain a better perspective on how grief was affecting my life and why it would well up, in a sense, without my thinking about it. Why now at this moment, and not in another? Why so strong a feeling of grief now and nothing at other times? Why a torrent of emotion and emptiness in one stroke and calm in another?

## *Tide*

To begin with, let me explain why the concept of tides. Tides are a recurrent pattern in our world. They are predictable to some extent, and yet they are not precise. They are recurrent because every day they rise, and they fall twice; there are two high tides and two low tides. They are predictable, but not precise, and they are variable.

The time for each tide changes every day, as well as how high and low the tides will be. This is because the position of the moon around the earth changes each day and affects the tide. It is also in relation to the sun. So that the position of the moon around the earth in relation to the position of both earth and moon to the sun affects the tides. That means that each month there is a cycling of the tides. Such that high tides vary in height and low tides vary in depth. The highest tides are when the moon is lined up with the sun, either by being on the same side of the earth or on the opposite side.

In all of this, there is one more factor. Apparently, the way the earth rotates around the sun can cause another effect every eighteen years when the way all things line up can create higher tides than normal, which are called super tides. Tides that can be several feet above normal levels and cause flooding.

There is one more factor of interest: where you are on the earth will affect the tides. Some places have much higher tides than others. In Panama, we see this. On the Caribbean side, high tides reach about one meter, but on the Pacific side, they can reach eight meters.

Now, what does this have to do with grief? Let me explain.

Our lives have routines to them. Those routines have not stopped just because of the loss of a loved one. Those routines have several patterns that affect us and our new cycles of life. There are daily, weekly, monthly cycles. And there are larger cycles, many of which we are unaware.

Before they were just like the tides, they came and went with regularity and we gave them little thought, but now that has changed. What we did together I now do alone. What the other person did, I now have to do without her and do it alone. What we did without them but shared later, we still do alone but no longer can share it with them, which accents the fact that we are alone.

To some extent, we find ways to deal with those events. We may find another person to share an activity, we may find someone to do what they did, and we may find someone with whom we can share what we have been doing. But only to some extent, because – one, they are not the same person; and two, there are some aspects in life where it is simply impossible to find someone to replace the person who has died. That and the fact that even when we find a person to take their place, it is never the same.

A friend, in a conversation about his remarriage and my wife's death, commented that I would never find one to replace my wife, but what I could find was a companion. I struggle with that idea because of the grooves in my life all those tides and movements have made. Will it be fair to that person to have to deal with that reality? That is a whole different topic, and maybe I will be ready to think about it farther down the road.

So, like the tides that come and go every day and follow their cycle, our activities come and go every day. We cook our food, do our work, wash our clothes, change the bed, and so on and so on. When everything goes smoothly, we may not even think about what has changed, but then one day we become sensitized to the rhythm and sense that there is a dissonance occurring, and we are struck again by what has changed. I cannot tell you exactly why this happens, but I can give you some ideas of things that can cause the flux in our reaction.

- It is the day of the month when the person died.
- We had a conversation with someone that triggers our latent grief.
- We talked about a topic that reminds us of who is missing.
- We do something, and they are not there to listen to us.
- We go somewhere, and when we return, they are not there to welcome us.

These are a few ideas of the triggers. Things that heighten our aware-ness of the grief in our life, like the position of the moon and sun in relation to the earth. And depending on just how much happens and how many triggers are affected, the emotion swells and fills us as it rushes in and then descends into a deeper sense of loss as it fades away and leaves one acutely aware of the loss.

Then there are times in the cycle that are stronger, special days like birthdays, anniversaries, and special celebrations that come less often but can create even greater swells in our emotions and sense of loss. The anni-versary of the person's death, or a unique combination of things, like the announcement of the birth of a grandchild for one who has lost a spouse. Or maybe the suggestion by a family member or close friend that maybe it is time to remarry and move on.

And like the different tides in different places, where we are in a giv-en time can have a similar effect of heightening our sensitivity. Visiting a place where we had special times together, being with family without that person, and any number of situations and settings can amplify the emo-tional issues and reduce our resistance and defenses.

Here is the key. If we don't know that this is normal and to be expected, like the tides, then we will flounder and be dragged under like a swimmer who is not paying attention and is caught in a riptide, a dangerous aspect of the movement of tides. We will be dragged under by the emotions and without clarity of thinking or the help of others who are very observant, we can find ourselves at great risk emotionally.

Well, that is the regular routines of life and grief. A tidal flow of emo-tions that will always be with us to a lesser or greater degree, depending on the effect of other factors on our life.

## Rogue Wave

The next word I used above is a rogue wave. A rogue wave is an unusually large wave, big enough to sink large ships. A regular large wave can reach ten meters (30+ ft.). These are usually part of large storm systems like ty-phoons and hurricanes. A rogue wave can reach thirty meters (100 ft.) and has been known to sink large ships because of their destructive force and unexpected arrival.

A rogue wave does not need a storm for it to come into existence, but that can be a factor. Other factors are things like winds, wave action, cur-rents, and underground terrain. The best known of the large waves are the waves off Hawaii that expert surfers desire to surf. These waves are caused by a combination of tide levels, winds, ocean currents, and the shape of the ocean bottom in that place.

These are predictable (in winter), and the surfers have a network set up to let them know when the biggest waves could occur so they can travel to Hawaii to surf them. Rogue waves are triple the size of these. With the large waves in Hawaii, you can choose if you will attempt them or not. And you will have access to information about all the dangers involved.

With a rogue wave, you cannot choose. A rogue wave can occur anywhere and at any time. A combination of events makes this wave possible. Unlike the big waves of Hawaii, these are much larger and usually only occur one at a time and are completely unpredictable. Unpredictable in that there is no way of seeing it until it is there, and you are battered by its incredible force. After it has passed, it is possible to reconstruct the events that made it possible. Things like current, wind, state of existing waves, etc. The reason for it being unpredictable is that it occurs in a fluid environment. Everything is in movement, and all at once, all the factors come together and create the wave. You have to be in the right place and the right time to see it. And in the emotionally fluid world of grief, we can be battered and bashed without warning. A series of events come together unexpectedly, and only when it has passed and has thoroughly thrashed us emotionally, do we see what caused the turmoil.

I am learning that there are times when my emotions run rampant, way out of control, or off the charts, in relation to what is happening in my life at that moment. While there may be some events I know can create emotional peaks, what I experience is so much more than what I am expecting. It is like several events have conspired to create a rogue wave that tears at me in its emotional energy. And when it has passed, I can see the elements that have created it. And then it has all changed, and knowing what has happened gives me no help in preparing for a repeat event because all the conditions will have changed. Remember, these are only ideas. Nothing in this list may be on your list of triggers and conditions needed for such an event.

What could contribute to such an event? Here are a few thoughts:

- Time of event
- Unexpected arrival of someone who has not yet dealt with your loss

- Death of another person under similar circumstances
- Dealing with the loss at some personal level not dealt with in the past
- Standing at the grave site after many years of absence
- A song that touches something buried deep within you

Remember, it is a combination of several things that occur at the same time that causes this huge swell of emotions. Such that it brings your life to a moment of pain at a level not seen previously in your grieving process. The last couple of weeks have felt like being hit by a rogue wave. Once while watching a very joyful music video called "Every Praise." It just crushed me. Hard to explain, but grief does that.

## Tsunami

The last one is the tsunami. This is not technically the same as the others. It is not based on anything regular or cyclic like the tides. And while the rogue wave is not regular or cyclic, it is based on things that are normal and cyclic that combine to have a greater impact. These two involve waves and movement of water based on patterns and cycles of water movement.

A tsunami is not. While it is a wave, its creation has another source. A sudden shift in the earth's crust creates a shock wave that moves immense amounts of water. This shock wave can travel thousands of miles undetected and only rise to the surface when it nears land. The shock wave then takes shape as a large movement of water that looks like a wave except in the amount of water being moved, the time in which the water is moved, and the cycle of repetition of the wave of water. A tsunami moves water in minutes as opposed to hours for a tide. It moves a vast amount of water, far beyond that of a normal tide, and it can repeat this movement several times in a matter of minutes and up to hours in between each surge.

One other thing. With tides and rogue waves, all the things that make up the event are found at that location at that moment. With a tsunami, this is not true. The water originally disturbed, which begins the process never arrives at the final location. The shock causes the water there to disturb the water next to it and continues transmitting it from one section to the next until water far from the site of the disturbances is released because it is the last in the chain reaction of events.

It is kind of like dominoes. You start the first one, which sets up the reaction until the last one moves. The key difference is that over time the number of dominoes being affected increases until a large number are being touched. Think of a pyramid of dominoes laid out horizontally. Each domino affects two, which affects four, and so on. The farther it goes, the greater the effect.

There can be many causes: underwater earthquakes, underwater landslides, volcanic eruptions, and a few other similar events. In each of these, the event and its effect are unpredictable in that you don't know when it will happen and where it will have the greatest effect. A big earthquake may have little effect, while a smaller one creates a devastating tsunami. A key feature is the remoteness of the two places from each other. The cause could be several thousand miles from where it finally arrives and creates what has often been called a tidal wave. Not totally accurate, but sufficient for this application.

To be honest, I have not experienced this level of emotion and struggle from grief, but it is there, and it is a real issue. An unrelated event triggers a sequence of events that touches the life of a grieving person and overwhelms them. And like a tsunami, there is little that can be done to prepare for such a catastrophic emotional event.

Maybe I shouldn't say an unrelated event. It may be better to say an event whose impact is multiplied far beyond normal because of who I am and what I have experienced. In psychology, they have a chart for emotional stress. Each major event in life has a designated stress factor. The highest three on this chart for stress are related to marriage, and the highest stress value is the death of a spouse (100). Fourth on the list is the death of a close family member (63), and then personal injury or illness (53). From there, they drop quickly to something like the stress of a vacation (13). Deciding your stress level at a given moment is looking at the list and totaling up the values of all the things happening in your life at a given moment. It is always a combination of things because one event usually triggers others or involves others.

Think about it this way. A rogue wave might create a sequence of events with a total of around 200 stress points. There are a lot of things that can combine to create this total. In my life, there was a moment when my total reached 215. They say that over 150 could cause serious health issues if not dealt with properly. Think of this as a rogue wave. But with the death of my wife and all the other changes, my total reached over 300. On the stress chart, the likelihood of having serious health issues is very high. Now imagine what might happen if suddenly one of my children or grandchildren died unexpectedly, or I became seriously ill. That and all the other stress factors would put me way over the limit and could create a tsunami of emotions and stress, each adding to each other in waves of increasing impact.

The key in all of this is the prior existence of my grief and how I have managed the stress involved in the grieving process. If I have done well then, the tsunami of emotion can be managed because of my experience and support structures and as a result, it may never form. If I have not done well in processing grief, then survival is going to be an issue.

Grief is a strange and complex emotion. I am still learning about how it has affected my life and has become a permanent part of who I am. I am learning that grief doesn't go away; we must learn how to live with it and use its presence to grow and move forward in life.

# Not What We Planned

A friend shared this phrase, *it is not what was planned,* about how the death of their spouse affected their life. Death will do that; change any plans you may have had in many areas of your life.

I am dealing with this in my life and in different areas from basic everyday stuff to the long-range planning we felt would be a great fit for our life, experience, and abilities.

The simplest plans were about our daily life. Nothing special, just to keep on enjoying each other's company, doing the work God had given us here, and living each day as it came. You know the mundane things of life that you plan to do: cook food, wash clothes, care for the house and anything that is on that list. You may not think much about it, but it is part of what you plan for and build your life around. And that planning was built around two people doing and sharing in it all.

Now it has all changed, and *it is not what was planned.*

Now I do all of that alone.

My wife was busy working on developing children's ministry at the church, helping develop an Internet café outreach ministry, and helping me with our training programs for missionaries and editing all the materials I was writing. She was great at involving me in those plans, and we looked forward each day to talk about what was happening and what needed to be done next.

I was busy traveling and teaching on a monthly basis. I was busy developing the resources and materials for my work and our work together in training. Plans were in place for joint trips and ministry in other places. When people came to our home to work on some of these projects, she became part of the process and cared for them so we could be effective in the work being done.

We enjoyed the planning and the challenges involved in this sharing together in all that was involved in these activities.

Now it has all changed, and *it is not what was planned.*

Except for one trip where my son took my wife's place, I do all that alone.

What we planned included regular contact with the kids, grandkids, and friends. We Skyped with them, chatted with them, and treasured the time with them, especially the grandchildren. We dreamed about when the next one would come and from which child. We thought about the next wedding, the next family event.

We talked about when and how each of us might be able to visit them. We looked at their schedules, planned Christmas events together. We made sure one of us would be able to be with them for special events. We talked about birthdays, anniversaries, and other special events and what to give each one. When traveling, there was always consideration given to what I could buy for them. Coffee, especially for one of them, jewelry for the daughters – for the one the weirder more unique, the better – and toys or something for the grandkids. Always planning that and how to get these gifts to them. We used visitors traveling back to states and other creative methods, or just storing it away to deliver the next time we saw them.

Now it has all changed, and *it is not what was planned.*

Now, all that has fallen to me. She kept a special calendar for all that stuff. She was always ready, and now I have this to plan and follow through on alone. Now there is only me to talk to.

We talked about our health and what we needed to do for her and me, for her health and treatment, to make sure she was getting all the care she needed for her cancer. We planned for it and worked our schedules around it so that I would be there when needed and she could travel as needed. We talked about my health. We planned for my checkups, so there would be no other surprises and issues to deal with.

We planned for continued options and many more years together one day at a time. We learned that important truth early on, and God gave us thirteen years of one day at a time.

Now it has all changed, and *it is not what was planned.*

There is no more discussion of treatments. There is no more need to plan around how she is feeling. And now if I have a need, she is not there for me.

We also looked down the road together at what our life and ministry could be like if we continued to receive one more day at a time. With our background and gifts, and the experience of living in so many places, we believed we would enjoy traveling to other countries for two to three months to help in teaching at a bible school, or other training programs. We looked forward to sharing all we had learned with others and helping them develop a deeper understanding of God's mission and the joy of serving.

We thought about being closer to the kids and grandkids and how we could spend more time with them. We thought about our home and about adding an all-season deck. We thought about all the things people entering retirement think about, hobbies and projects that we could enjoy and so on.

Now it has all changed, and *it is not what was planned.*

Many of the plans will still be possible, but not as a couple. Being closer to the kids and the grandkids and more a part of their lives is still a goal, but it will only involve me. That means the grandkids will only get to know their grandmother through the pictures and stories that will be shared by their parents and grandfather. The activities will change – not all, but many – because there is just me.

This phrase, *it is not what we planned*, carries a lot of baggage with it. So much of life is built around it. From daily activities to family relations, ministry plans, and on the list goes. And it is not an easy burden to deal with. That is because before there were *two* people to do the heavy lifting, planning, and follow-through. Now there is just one.

Some areas cannot be set aside. You will have to make changes to your plans in order to take care of all those daily activities, all those relationships with family and friends. Some aspects of your ministry will not change; you still have the work to do. At times you may have to fulfill joint commitments alone. At times you will have to let go of things because you can't do them alone. Not an easy decision.

When it comes to your personal areas of responsibility, there will be changes here as well. Before you had another person to encourage, counsel, and listen. Now you will have to adjust. There will still exist the influence and patterns from all the past that you can use, and that is a great comfort. But it will not fully replace what is no longer present, and the way you plan and carry out those plans will change.

If that is not enough the toughest thing of all about *not what was planned* is that each day you will get up and face another day that is *not what was planned*, and at the end of the day you go to bed alone, and that may be the toughest reminder that *it is not what was planned.*

It sounds difficult; actually, it is not just difficult, it may seem impossible to deal with. When a person who loses their spouse wakes up, that is the reality. *It is not what was planned* and the emotional stress can be crushing. What needs to be clear is that it is a normal part of the process of grief.

It will take time to work through all the adjustments and growth needed so that a new plan can take shape. A plan that adapts to what has happened and all the changes that need to take place in *what was planned.* There are no secrets in this process. There are sources of help in family, friends, coworkers, and others that God brings alongside. Like people who have been through the process. A key will be the depth of your relationship with God, but that should be obvious, and many books have been written to help those dealing with grief and explain all that God provides to bring peace and joy back into your life.

But, if I am going to be honest, if I don't accept the fact that life *is not what was planned* and learn how to adapt and live in this new environment without my spouse, I will die and fade away. I will live in a world of perpetual mourning for something that cannot be restored. I will try to create a life that cannot be maintained.

So be honest and say it with clarity, "This is not what was planned," and begin to look for what can happen in your life because of all that was planned. Learn that all of what was planned will give you incredible resources and foundations that you can build on to keep on living and planning without losing the blessings of what you had planned and thought of before your partner died. And if done right, it will allow others to fill those areas where it takes more than one to move forward.

Yes, *it is not what was planned*, but now there is a new opportunity to plan. An opportunity to use what you did as a couple, use the past lessons to build a future direction, and in so doing, honoring that and sharing that blessing with others.

# Not What I Planned

I am discovering that there is a flip side to the idea of *it is not what was planned,* and that is *it is not what **I** planned.*

Before the death of my wife, all my thoughts and planning included another person. This included how our time, work, and finances were organized, and other areas. Now everything has shifted, and the planning related to time, work, and finances have changed.

Let me start with time. Now I don't have to think about the time I will spend with my wife and what she does with her time in relation to us. It is just not needed. This means that it may appear that I have more time available to do what I need or want to do. But there is a trade off here. Now I need to set aside time for the things she did to free me to do the work I need to do. The time set aside to work together on a project or activity.

Now I have to do all of what she did, and if both of us were involved in the activity, allow more time to be able to do the activity or work that required the involvement of two people. An example would be painting the house. We both had our areas of responsibility, which reduced the workload for each of us. Now I have to plan for all the work and then do it all. While I have gained time, in one respect, that same time must be reevaluated to be able to complete what used to be a joint task. In the end, I don't really gain any time.

This is not something I planned for in the past but now must plan for from now on. And this has nothing to do with who did what but the fact that I must plan to do all of what is needed instead of sharing the work and responsibility with another.

That brings us to the area of work, which is affected in various ways. This is mainly because we worked together on my projects, or she was a key resource and helped in what I was doing. As a result, my work was often planned around her or dependent on her involvement.

All that has changed, and she is no longer part of what I plan related to the work I do. Now I have to do all the work she helped with and make plans to involve others in key areas. That is *not what I planned.*

My wife had unique skills that enhanced what I did, and I had unique skills that allowed her to accomplish her plans and goals. Because we knew what each other could do and how each could help, we planned our work accordingly. Now I must plan my work without that input and no longer can be part of what she was doing. Now I no longer have access to her skills. I no longer have a built-in critic and editor, for example. One who understood how I think and work and knew how to make suggestions and changes when and where necessary.

Now I must plan the work differently and search for others to help. But that takes more time and affects my planning. That means I may have to adapt to the planning, availability, and structure of the lives of others. Something that is *not what I planned.*

These are somewhat obvious. It happens throughout our life. Changes that affect you and become not what you planned for and cause you to start a new planning cycle. Here are a few examples:

- when you leave the home of your parents to live as a single,
- when you get married, which definitely changes how you do planning,
- when children become part of your life and leave your life, another change in what you plan for.

Those are fairly natural and expected, and though you cannot fully plan for the change in planning, it is anticipated, and we often have the help of others, if we desire. *It is not what I planned* exactly, but I was planning for the change at some level.

There is another set of changes, changes that are sudden and impossible to anticipate: major illness, disaster, or accidents. These quickly bring change. The impact of each is different, but each requires you to change your plans. The change is more manageable when there are two or more involved. But when it is the loss of a spouse, especially after all the kids are gone, it becomes more challenging. All you planned together is now erased, and now you must deal with it alone.

Now you are dealing with *not what I planned.*

Now we are ready for the last area of *not what I planned*, what happens in relation to finances. It follows the ideas of the previous areas in that there will be changes. There will be changes in your finances, and you will now deal with it by yourself and not with the involvement of another person.

Before, you budgeted according to the needs of two people. Before, your planning had to provide food for two, clothing for two, cost of transport for two, and so on. The change from two to one means that there may be more money available than before. At least at some level. And you didn't plan for this in so many ways. (I will need to admit that in some cases, if life was dependent on joint income, this may not be true. That creates some differences, but the issue is the same. I have to plan differently. I will deal with the prior concept.)

For me, there was a change in income. It dropped at one level, but it was replaced by several other things that occurred. Because we had planned for the future and possible death of one of us, a far distant future, we purchased life insurance. I received those payments after she died. That meant I had the funds I needed to clear several key debts. I also, because of our ages, began receiving a monthly check from the government. This meant that with the debts gone and the extra income, I did indeed have more funds available to do a number of things.

I could buy the things I needed for the house. I could buy better quality items. I had more freedom to travel and take a vacation. I could be more generous (something my wife made possible and sought to do whenever possible). I even could take care of some much-needed upkeep and repair to our house, which was a challenge before and would have involved some kind of financial planning. Now I had the funds to do it without borrowing.

But as I did what I had not planned to do, I encountered a struggle that caught me off guard. It went like this: I bought or did something, and then I thought my wife would have appreciated this, that this would have made my wife's responsibilities easier, or she would have enjoyed doing this. The worst was when I bought something that I had really wanted but there had been no funds for, things that would make my work easier, more efficient, and better. As I thought about this, I was stricken by a wave of *how selfish you are*. And if I chose to buy something just for me, I struggled with *how could you do that with the funds received because of her death?*

At this point, the *not what I planned* became a bit of a struggle. I am slowly coming to terms with this idea, but not without some discomfort. It is easier to deal with this when others besides me can benefit. It is easier when it helps me do a better job of reordering my time and work. It is easier when I know that she would, in fact, have been pleased with what I have decided and maybe enjoyed having it or doing what I planned, and when I know that if we had had the money we would have bought, paid for, or budgeted for it. But only easier. There is still a feeling of guilt and I sense that it will take some time to process that completely.

*Not what we planned* is part of the process. If I don't deal with that, I may not be able to adequately deal with *not what I planned*, but in fact must plan. Not dealing with the one can make it hard to understand and learn how to handle the other.

The emotions will be more intense if what you plan is something that both of you had planned, such as a purchase, an activity, or a trip that you must now do alone. I use *must* because sometimes that is exactly what happens. For me, one trip will be to see our new grandchild, something that only I will be able to do; a *not what **we** planned* now becomes *not what **I** planned*.

I could give many examples. The truth is that now everything will become *not what I planned*. And to move healthily into this means being very honest with what I feel. And learning to identify what is happening – the sadness, guilt, frustration, loneliness and other difficult emotions – so I can find the correct way to handle what is happening as I deal with this is *not what I planned* in relation to time, work, finances, and any other area that will be affected by this truth.

# Descent into Oblivion

My entire world is disappearing around me. It feels like I am descending into oblivion, lost from thought and sight.

At some point in the process of loss and mourning, this feeling will come. It is because my identity as a couple is slowly being eroded, erased, even rewritten by myself and those around me. It is a strange feeling.

Eroded, because day by day the changes that occur, because my wife has died, slowly eat away at what was. It is like the action of a river or of rain. Day by day, it passes by, removing material from the bank and carrying it away. Soil is easily removed from banks made of dirt. Just go down to the river and see where a tree has fallen into the river. That is the testimony of the erosion. Even rock can be eaten away. Waterfalls are the most obvious example of this: at the bottom are always rocks that have fallen as the water eats away until one falls. Rain can erode surfaces to carry away what it touches.

My life is filled with actions and events that work to remove what was and carry it away. Little by little, people stop referring to *us* and only to *me*. It is no longer Perry and Nancy it is just Perry. Sometimes the process is faster, changes in documents and legal papers. Sometimes it is slower. Some people just don't stop referring to me in the you plural. But over time it happens. What always represented *us* now only represents *me*. And what was the life of a couple descends slowly into oblivion.

It is never quite lost. It is a slow descent, but a descent nonetheless. And it is impelled by another factor: all the new people that come into my world only know me and have never met my wife. This further erodes the image of a couple and replaces it with a single entity: me.

"Erased" is a stronger word. But it does happen. We, in some situations and contexts, erase aspects of the past. Is it because our memory banks are overloaded, and we need space for new information? Is it because the information is no longer relevant, and so like an old file, we put it in the trash bin and then hit empty?

It is a frustrating thing and sometimes we fight the process. We don't want to forget. Well, let's be clear about this: there is a lot I don't want to forget, but there is always something a person prefers to forget. Life is not perfect, and what was not perfect we want to erase. We want to keep in our active memory the best image possible.

Unfortunately, erasing is easy and not just of less-than-desirable memories. It is said we can recall everything or almost everything. Our brain has an incredible storage capacity. But at the same time, it attaches levels of importance to information. The least important is barely recoverable and, in a sense, erased. I saw this over and over. My wife would remember things I couldn't and I the same for her. If we talked long enough, kind of like the work of a recovery program, I could recall pieces of what she remembered.

I also see this again as I write a series of letters or anecdotes of our life. Fortunately, I have a very large collection of letters written by her and thousands of photos to help me restore what was erased. I am sure if you have anything like that, you will know what I mean. A memory has been forgotten, erased, but with the use of key triggers, it can be partially recovered.

The thing is that this happens in the present. Your emotions and how you process them affect this, and without realizing it you erase things from active memory. It could be because of the painful nature of the memory, the context of the situation, too many emotions, and whatever was happening – and it is gone. It can be just the process of mourning and moving on in life that causes you to erase one memory to make room for the new.

I can imagine this happening more if I decide to remarry. I will need to erase some past to make room for what is new. If I don't, I may not be able to enter the new. The past will create problems for the new information unless I erase it. It must pass into oblivion.

It is a scary concept for me at this moment. Yet I see it happening. I am letting the new experiences of my life replace certain aspects of the past, and it cannot be stopped. Your body does it all the time, replacing old cells with new to keep you strong. Aging occurs when that process is not effective. Emotional health is the same, I think. If we don't replace old memories with new, we will become trapped in the past and unable to live in the present or have the will to live in the future.

Look around you, and you will find those people. The most obvious is the person with Alzheimer's. They only have the past, and that is where they live. But that is a disease or breakdown of normal functions. But some people choose to live like that. Their whole world is lived in the past, and they pass into oblivion because they are not with us in the present.

In a sense, one of two things will happen: either certain aspects of your life must be erased and pass into oblivion in order to function in the present, or you as a person will descend into oblivion, out of touch with the world around you.

The last idea is maybe the most disturbing, rewriting the transcript of events. In a way, it is a natural desire. We want to gloss over the negative and only keep the positive, and so we rewrite the story. It is quite a temptation. The reason we do this? I don't know exactly, but I can think of a few, and they are tempting to me as well.

Idolize the person. My wife was the most incredible person. She could do no wrong, she always had the right attitude, and she always knew what to do. To be honest, there is a level at which I believe this of my wife. She was incredible. But she was no more perfect than I am and struggled with attitude issues and knowing what to do just like me.

Create a role model. If you want an example of how to live and serve, my wife is the perfect example. And as we share the information, we manage to leave out the struggles, well not all the struggles, only the ones that would mar the image of a perfect role model.

My wife fought cancer for thirteen years and became a role model for others who were struggling. She was a fighter and refused to let the cancer define her life and ministry. But she also had her days of struggle, and so did I. It was in those days we both learned how to live each day in the strength of God.

Unfortunately, many people don't want to hear about the struggles and failures that were part of life and that created the role model others wanted to see. That makes it tempting to rewrite the story and remember mainly the victories. No war is won without ever experiencing defeat along the way.

Avoid the painful memories. These can be past and present, even future. We don't want to be reminded of a painful memory, so we rewrite the story just a little so as to reduce our pain and be able to deal with the present. We are struggling with the loss in the present, and so we do a little creative editing so others don't know what is happening inside. Only those who are close have even a chance at detecting the editing that is happening.

It takes the form of, *I am fine, and here is what I am doing to prove that I am fine.* Except what I am doing is designed to rewrite the reality so that I attempt not only to fool you but also myself into believing it is in fact fine. There are other phrases: I am managing; I keep moving forward, I am learning to go on. The problem is that they can be true or be used to rewrite the reality of what is happening in my heart and soul.

I don't want to deal with it, so I rewrite it.

As to the future, believe it or not, we can do the rewriting of the future. We design the story before it happens and then live it. Instead of letting life happen and dealing with real-time living and all its emotions, failures, and challenges, we rewrite it to avoid all that might cause pain. We rewrite it to avoid traveling down difficult paths, dealing with difficult encounters, and facing the reality of our loss.

In each of these, the truth descends into oblivion. In some, it is a healthy process. We need to let go of some aspects of past, present, and possible future in order to live. In others, it is a dangerous response that may cause me more harm than the possible protection from the pain I imagine I will receive.

I am in a descent into oblivion. The hope is that what arises will be an amalgamation of all that was good of my marriage, my love for my wife, and the person it created. Something that will give me greater strength to face each day and the changes I will need to make.

# Background Static

There is always in the background of life what is called static. The newer generation might not be as familiar with this concept because so much has been done to clean up our sound on all the things we use: TVs, radio, and many other electronic communication devices. We are all familiar with the idea of a poor signal and how it breaks up our communication, but that is not static. Poor signals impede the flow of the sound or the image.

Static is just there in the background making noise. If it is strong enough, it becomes the predominant sound forcing what you want to hear to the background. When it is weak, it is hardly noticed, but it is still there.

There are different ways to reduce the static in communication. One is, do a better job of tuning in the signal you want to hear, which eliminates much of the static, but never all of it. It is still there, just much weaker. Another method is to apply filters to remove or mask the sound. Most audio video software has these kinds of filters. To work they remove certain frequencies with the intent or hope that in doing so the static again may be reduced. It often works but can affect the quality of the communication that is left. A third option is to boost the gain or sound level of what you want to hear. The intent here is to drown out or overcome the static in order to hear what is desired, or at least to make it more audible. Unfortunately, the static can become more noticeable in the process as well.

There is a common thread in each of these, and it makes sense, at least in the realm of audiovisual communication. The static interferes with what we want to hear. The better we do at removing it or overcoming it, the better we can see and hear what is being broadcast.

Think of it this way. You are trying to talk to someone in a crowded room or place where there is a lot of activity. That noise makes it a challenge to hear. And sometimes, if the lighting is poor, to even see who is talking and be able to see the non-verbal aspect of the communication. If the communication is critical enough, more than casual comments and conversation, you will work at reducing the interference. You could find a quieter better-lit environment. You could find a different time when there is less noise. You can even speak louder to be heard, if you don't want to take the time and effort to use the previous options.

This is all normal, and the normal way we think of static. But I am learning there is another kind of static that is part of our world. It is a background noise that impinges on our thoughts and activities. It is a subtle reality that can surface when we least expect it. But it can also surface when we intentionally encourage it to be present. And like the static above, we can choose how to react to it by either dampening, masking, or even amplifying it, depending on what is happening and how we perceive this static.

This static can be negative, neutral, and positive. It can create an ambiance of introspection, contentment, and pleasure, as well as distraction, frustration, and annoyance. A lot depends on why it exists and what is happening in our life and emotions at that moment.

This static is made up of several factors. It is made up of our experiences, emotions, and attitudes. It is built on the nature of our relations, good and bad. It is deeply linked to our memories and our hopes and desires. And it is clearly tied to the gains and losses in our lives, especially when there is a loss of a spouse.

It is this loss that has made me aware of this static that is now part of my world, the reality of the ongoing presence of my relationship with my wife, who is now gone. At least she is physically gone, but the noise, the sound of her presence, her static in my world, continues. It is something that I doubt will ever go away and I am not sure it would be a good idea to completely rid my world of the background noise that she creates in my world.

Let me try to explain what I mean. At least some of what this means.

As I travel, I encounter people who knew my wife. She was the type of person who could quickly and easily impact people profoundly and positively. So, when I meet them, they comment on that impact and how much they appreciated her (to be honest I have yet to meet someone who has been affected negatively). As a result, the background noise of our life and marriage increases in volume.

As I do things around the house, I find myself caught up, without intent or plan, in thinking about what she would or would not do in relation to what I am doing – thinking about what she would like or dislike in that moment, thinking about how our world functioned as a couple, thinking these thoughts and so many other things. Again, the background static of her presence has become apparent and almost palpable to me.

Even when I am planning future activities, her influence is present. It may relate to following through on something we had started or dreamed of starting. It may be totally unrelated, and yet her desires, dreams, and person become a tangible factor in what I am planning or envisioning.

This is not a surprise, or it shouldn't be. When two people have lived together for almost forty years, that is how life functions. It is a good thing because it keeps your perspective open to the opinions and recommendations of others. It helps you learn to see things from another person's perspective as well as your own. Again, a good thing, a real blessing as one moves forward. It is consoling to know that in this sense I can still depend on what we learned together and what we have enjoyed continuing to function and provide me the ability to keep my thoughts and plans open. I can still draw on her perspective because it is still there in the form of background static.

Now you may wonder why I am using the idea of background static. It makes it sound like a negative thing, something that could impact my ability to hear other sounds and clearly hear the other information around me, the music, communication, and visual images that will continue to enter my life. Static does have the connotation of being interference and not helpful.

And that is the point. The background static of my relationship with my wife can become a distraction, noise, interference, and even become so loud as to drown out the messages I could receive from others. Or it can create a distortion in the signals I receive from others, resulting in misinterpretation of purpose and intent. That kind of distortion can result in people not wanting to be part of my life and avoiding me. It can be of such a nature that I will mistrust them, offend them, and avoid them and they me.

Managed correctly, this background static can enhance the quality of what is received. It would be like music used to enhance times of thought and meditation, music that allows a greater appreciation of what I am hearing, creating an ability to interpret and respond more effectively.

The background static that occurs when we deal with loss can have so much potential to help a person as they move forward in the new condition of life as well as be a source of greater struggle and pain. It all depends on how we use it and the effect we allow it to have on those around us and our relationship to those people who continue to be part of our life and those who will enter our life as we move forward. I have many choices to make and much to learn about how to value it properly, and in that process, to learn how to control the volume and intensity, so to speak, of its presence in my thoughts, plans, and relationship.

Sometimes this will be easy, because those around me want to see and hear that background as we meet and interact. Sometimes it will be a challenge as I learn how it may affect the new situations and relationships that will develop in the days ahead. Too loud and it will overwhelm, too soft and I will lose something valuable that I need to keep my balance.

I wish I knew exactly how to do that in every situation. I don't. I have to be alert to every situation, every person, and every context. Over time, I will begin to learn at what level I need to allow it to be played. A key will be having people around me who I know will be honest enough to help me see if and when it gets too loud or too soft.

This background static will not go away. I cannot erase almost forty years of life. I cannot erase the fact that I have children who want to remember and see the place their mother has in my world and theirs. That is not a wise thing to do. And I must not play it too loudly, so loudly that it drowns out the new memories that want to develop and add to what is already playing. It is like a music score that is being written. The wise composer knows when to keep the theme prominent and when to let it fade to the background as a new movement and interpretation are added to create not a simple score but a symphony.

So, I am dealing with the background static and learning to write a new movement to the symphony of my life that enhances and is enhanced by what has already been written.

# Dead Calm, Vacuum, and Deafening Roar

A dead calm is when there is no wind, nothing that will fill the sails so a ship can move. It is a dangerous situation. It is so dangerous that if it lasts too long, food and water supplies begin to run out. It is so dangerous that a ship caught in it was known to try to use rowboats to pull the ship clear – not an easy task when you consider the size difference and that there are only a few men trying to pull everyone and everything else.

Emotional dead calms occur. There is no movement, no ability to move. You are locked in place by what has happened and feel like you are frozen in time. The thing is, you know exactly where you are, but you are caught in a trap with no escape.

Day by day your emotional resources are sapped, and desperation can set in. The problem is the more you fight the situation, the more you sap your energy. It is like that rowboat whose men are struggling to move the much larger object. To do so they will expend more energy, need more rest and more water, thereby further depleting those resources – with little or no success.

Fighting it doesn't work. But there is something that will pull you free in time. The ocean is filled with currents. The wind may have stopped but there is a subtle flow that pulls everything with it. In time, if you are wise in using your resources and can avoid overreacting you will finally be free. It is not easy to wait for something other than your efforts to accomplish what needs to be done but that is the secret.

With the loss of someone dear, like a spouse, we can easily find ourselves trapped in the emotions of the moment, barely functional. If not at first, at some point there will be a feeling of a loss of direction and the impossibility of moving beyond the moment. A feeling of being hemmed in and cut off. There is no wind, which means no rain, no clouds, and no relief.

The attempts to gain control only sap your energy and create a deeper need and heighten your weakness to face the danger and do what is necessary.

So often, the best solution is not to fight what is happening. It is best to engage in the reality of the moment and let it provide the strength and patience needed to wait for a breeze, and the faith to believe that there are currents and movements in the form of friends, scriptures, and your relationship with God that are at work to draw you out of the dead calm of what has happened.

How long does it take? I wish I knew. Will it only happen once? Not likely. Is there a way to avoid this? Not a wise thing to do. Will I know where my help comes from? Maybe, but only if you are not fighting and so blinding yourself to the help that is there.

It is a frightening thing to find oneself stuck emotionally and spiritually. What is more frightening is what happens when a person does not understand what is happening and all their efforts simply extend the time in which they are caught in the dead calm. There are questions to ask: Will I be willing to let it all process and, in time, move me out of that moment? Will I let the natural currents of life do their work and carry me forward?

A vacuum is the absence of atmosphere. I use the word "atmosphere" because you can have a vacuum devoid of air, water, and many other gases and substances. Vacuum can apply to a complete lack of anything that normally should be present, but has been removed until nothing is left of that substance in the space occupied by a vacuum.

We often talk about the vacuum of space and how it is devoid of an atmosphere, yet it is not totally devoid of everything. It is filled with gravity, light, and the movement of submicroscopic particles and other unseen items.

So, a vacuum cannot be in truth the complete absence of everything, but is, in fact, the absence of a specific substance. A substance that is absolutely necessary for something to exist or function. Are you understanding what I am saying?

When my wife died, I entered a vacuum. The complete absence of her physical presence. The complete absence of her verbal communication. The complete absence of so many things related to our marriage and life together. In that moment, they were all gone. Even more difficult is that they could not be restored.

A vacuum involving the removal of the atmosphere is the same. You may place atmosphere in the container again, but it is not the same atmosphere as what you took out. You might say that light and gravity would be the same, but if you understand physics, they are not. You can't recall the light that has passed or bring back the gravity wave that was removed. Don't ask me the physics of the thing. It is beyond me, but that is what they say.

In the same way, what has happened in your life, the vacuum of loss and what was removed, can never be restored. And while people try all manner of things to create the illusion that what was lost is back, displaying photos of the one who has died, maintaining all the daily routines exactly as they have always been, and many more. It just doesn't work. A picture doesn't replace the person, keeping the routine does not keep them alive, except in our thoughts. And while doing those things is not bad, it will not return what was lost.

I am living in that vacuum. My wife is gone. The routines of life are lost. And the pictures, and all the other stuff, will not restore the vacuum created to what it was before the vacuum occurred. In time, I may replace what is gone. I will develop new relationships, new routines, and healthy ways to remember what was removed from my life to create the vacuum.

The questions are: Will I let go of what I cannot recover and move on to truly enjoying the memories and blessings of the life we had? Will I do what is healthy in the way of remembering and slowly refilling the container with positive emotions and relations, while at the same time not staining the container's outside with attempts to paint it all over and create a false image? If I do so, I am only fooling myself and not allowing myself to heal and refill the vacuum with what is needed for me to honor my wife and live again.

The last concept is the deafening roar, a sound so intense you can't hear anything else. It is like the great rock concerts with their mountains of speakers all set to the absolute limit, a limit so high you can't hear anything else, with the volume so high that over time you will damage your ability to hear the finer sounds and their subtleties: a bird chirping, the ripple of a brook, a whisper, and more. The subtle sounds are all lost because you have been deafened by a roar of sound over and over and over.

Why do you think people who work with jackhammers and other loud machines use headphones? They do so because if they don't, at the end of the day, they can hardly hear anything below a shout. And who wants to have someone always shouting at them? The saddest part of this is how many deny they are having trouble hearing.

The death of a loved one does that to a person. The roar of the emotions and tears becomes so loud that nothing else can be heard. No one's kind words are heard, no one's attempt to bring solace are heard. Don't talk to me because I don't want to hear. That is what we say, but what is really happening is that we have turned up the volume of our emotions so high that we can't hear. And when it finally does get turned down, we are deaf to any further attempts to speak to us and try to bring an element of comfort into our lives. We just can't hear what people are saying

There is also the roar of emptiness. It is amazing how loud silence can sound when you are expecting to hear something else and there is nothing. No clatter of pans in the kitchen preparing the meal, no knock at the door to say it is ready, no quiet conversation about the day. These are the deafening silence in my world. You may have others. I find it especially loud when I return from a trip and no one is there to greet me, look at my pictures, and talk about how her days and mine went.

The biggest danger is filling this deafening roar with anything. You can play their favorite music over and over in an attempt to fill the silence, but for some reason, your ability to turn up the volume is never enough to drown out the deafening roar of that silence.

It is better to just listen to it and let the silence itself provide access to the wonderful memories and times together and the way to move on. Easy to say, hard to do, but so necessary. Because if you get trapped in this deafening silence, you will never hear what good thing God may have to say to you. You don't want to hear because you think it means abandoning those pleasant sounds. And to a certain extent, that will happen. Those sounds will not come back.

So, you choose, let the past drown out any beautiful message or sound of the future, or open your heart to a blending of the two. Something special that lets you enjoy all that has been and receive the blessing of all that will be.

Let me be honest. It is easy to write this down. It is another thing to work it all out. For some, it may happen quickly, and for others, years. For me, I expect some things to happen quicker and others to take years to process and bring about a healthy change. That is all right as long as I know what is happening and I am actively part of doing what needs to be done to escape the dead calm, refill the vacuum, and learn to shut down the deafening roar so I can hear the beauty around me.

# Mourning – Dealing with Loss, Grief, and Renewal

Mourning is the process of expressing what has happened to a person when there is a significant change in their life. A loss that creates changes that cannot be avoided nor permit simple actions to overcome those changes.

Many words are used in describing mourning and the processes involved. The two most obvious are the words found in the title. The first is loss. Many times people, in dealing with the death of a person in another's life use a simple phrase, *I am sorry for your loss.* I have seen this phrase used over and over in situations where a person, family, friend, or even stranger uses it as a means of starting a conversation.

What is often interesting is that it is not always used as a way to enter into a conversation about the loss that has occurred but rather as a means to identify the loss and move on to other issues and aspects of life and what is happening. For the most part, those who have not actually experienced the loss want to move on to other areas more comfortable or more relevant to their life.

For those who are directly affected, like the family of the person, and those who were very close to the person the phrase is of little use. You don't see a son talking to his father about the death of their mother/wife in this manner. The loss is much more personal and real. Instead of it being your loss it is my loss. I lost my wife, my sibling, my parent, my best friend, and so on.

And you mourn that reality. You have lost something that cannot ever be replaced. Let's be clear about this. Others may enter your life and fill the role or aspects of what has been lost, but that never replaces what was lost. That loss has a specific name, a specific time frame, and specific results in my life. Another person cannot enter into my memories and history the way the one who has died did. It is simple, it is because they were not there when it happened or were not an essential part of what happened.

They were not in any way part of the picture. And while the memory of the person's presence is still part of it, you cannot draw on the one you have lost to remember, to review, or do any of the things people do related to their history and shared experiences. You may be able to tell someone, and they may have had a similar experience, but it just isn't the same.

The loss is real and touches me at so many levels. Levels that are evident, levels that are profound, and levels that are hidden and only realized over time. As a result, when people talk to me about my loss I don't enter into the discussion. Often, not always, they are only thinking at a basic level of loss. The person is gone. Me, I am living at a whole different level. The person is gone, and they took with them more than I can understand and explain.

As you can see, mourning a loss is much more complicated. On day one, all one can see is the absence of the person, their physical presence. But then begins a sequence or series of events that unravels the reality, and the loss becomes so much more. At this point, the mourning changes as the deeper reality of what has been lost grows and grows. It can easily become overwhelming in its immensity. So much so that people become frozen, unable to function at almost any level.

They wander around lost, like zombies, simply acting out the routines of life. And each routine activity accents the loss and deepens the impact of loss in life. Mourning now becomes as much the loss of the person as all that they represent in my life.

Grief is about the physical anguish we experience and how we express the loss. It doesn't matter if it results in absolute silence and stoic behavior or incredible wailing and physical expression. Both represent the fact that I am reacting to what has happened.

Grief has a wide range of expressions, as noted above. It also has quite a process that it can go through. It has the ability to morph, to change over time. Grief can be very physical in nature, wailing, emotional outbursts, crying without reason, and on the list goes. Grief can create depression, isolation, and even the opposite – a person reacts to grief by becoming overly active, involved in everything.

Grief may result in constant expressions of the pain and loss. It may do just the opposite and create false fronts to hide behind. People think they are hiding from the grief, the pain, but what is happening is they are internalizing it. They are attempting to control the grief and put on a bold face for all to see. But grief will find a way to be expressed, eventually. And those who think they can control it are not capable of judging the results. Such control comes at a cost and will touch one's relationships and change their normal behavior. That is because to control the grief requires that.

I chose not to fight my grief. I am not a man who cries, but I realized that I needed that release, intense release, in order to have any real emotional balance. I chose not to hide away but to respond to those I believed wanted to hear what was happening in my world. One friend, as he listened to me remembering a past visit to his house with my wife, looked at me and said I was still in mourning, still grieving the loss.

At first, I wasn't sure what he meant, but slowly it became clear. Grief has many elements. The most obvious are those that are evident and quite visible, the emotions. But others are not so expressive. They are the stories we tell of the past. The stories and memories that relate to where I am and what is happening at the moment that have links to the past.

This is a good expression of grief. And it will remain beneficial as long as you don't get stuck in the story process. It is like anyone who retells over and over and over an event, an accomplishment, a memory, until the entire world has heard and is tired of hearing it again. Proper grief knows when it is time to stop crying in public, to stop sharing information of the past, and to begin processing it all and making it possible to move forward.

I am still mourning. Some of it is because I keep meeting people who have not had the chance to say how sorry they are, not just the, "I am sorry for your loss." People who knew us as a couple and shared a unique time or event with us as a couple. They need a chance to grieve and I need to let it happen. It is good for them and me. I am still mourning because I am still encountering new situations that remind me of the loss and all that has changed. I am still mourning because enough time has not passed yet since my wife died.

When will this stop? I am not sure. In some ways, I will never stop mourning. The anniversaries of her death, our marriage, her birthday, and other key events will continue to be repeated. They will continue to remind me of the loss. What will need to stop is my need for others to be caught up in it, at least others not personally affected by the source of my grief. I expect my kids will deal with this in their own way for a while.

I see it in the comments that come on social media and other sources. Out of nowhere, someone will comment about how they miss my wife. It will be about something she did for them, something they shared together, or other events. It will remind me of my grief and cause me to pause.

There will be triggers that bring it back to the surface – a song, a meal, a birthday of a child or grandchild – and again I am dealing with my grief.

All of this is okay. It is when it takes control and affects more than that moment, when it becomes the focus of my life. It's when I won't let go of things that are sure to keep me in a cycle of grief, or maybe there are things I use to keep my grief alive and fresh, as if I should never stop grieving in a public and outward manner.

Yes, grief is complicated, and it is very personal. If not accepted and allowed, it causes problems. If allowed to control and dominate, it will cause other problems. The key is, don't be afraid to grieve and then don't be afraid to say it is time to stop grieving and move on. And please don't ask me what I mean by moving on. I am not sure yet. But I am pretty sure it doesn't mean denial of my loss but involves an appropriate response to my grief that does not dominate my life or those around me.

If we do all this well, dealing with loss and learning how to handle grief, we will take the next step in the process of mourning. The next step is renewal. I am still working on this one. In fact, I am just barely entering the process of learning what life after grief can be.

I know for sure it will involve redefining my relations with those around me. It will involve learning how to relate to my kids, grandkids, and extended family as an individual and not as a couple. Mom is not there. Grandma is gone. It means learning not to say too many times, "Mom would have loved this," and "It's too bad grandma is not here to . . ." A few of those are all right. But renewal involves moving beyond that and being the one to enjoy and experience the moment without the regret or reminder of who is not there. It will take time. At first, it will involve learning to be quiet, then focusing on what is happening in the moment, and beginning to look forward to those times because they are mine to enjoy.

Renewal will involve developing new activities and friendships. It will also mean learning how to enjoy what I used to do as a couple, as a single. It is possible, but it takes time and a willingness to process the grief and realizing it is all right to enjoy this alone. Slowly, it may be possible to bring others into those areas. They will never have the same appreciation and involvement. That is all right. What they can bring is new ideas, new focuses, new ways of experiencing and enjoying that activity. A good thing.

Renewal involves a slow process of letting key people behind the facade. Yes, we have to admit that to live, for a while, we create a facade. Something so that people see us as normal, both those who are new to our world and others who have been a part of our world. This is not about sharing the secrets and special stuff from the past, but about allowing them inside to create a new story, new secrets (things that only exist where there are true and healthy relationships), and new special stuff.

I use vague terms because I don't know what they are. But you will know as you let your life be renewed and begin to believe that you can really come up for air and breathe again, deep refreshing breaths of life and possibilities. Renewal is finding that you can live again and there is room in your world for others who can fill some, not all, of what has been missing since your loss.

Renewal will allow you to create new ways of dealing with the events and relations that will happen and become part of your life. It will create space in your heart, soul, and mind for the unknown that lies ahead, and you will not be afraid to take the risks to move forward and go into the future.

Mourning is quite a process. Handled badly it will destroy you and those around you. Handled properly it will release you and provide what you need to be restored and renewed, so you can once again live.

# The Vows Are Fulfilled

*For better or for worse*
*For richer or poorer*
*In sickness and in health*

These are part of the content of most wedding vows. The pastor tells each person to repeat after him, and the bride and groom in their turn repeat them and then say, "until death do us part."

These are what I promised to my wife, and she promised the same to me. It was a promise we both kept. We lived and loved each other through all that happened in our marriage. We were there to help each other when life was a struggle and even dangerous to us and our family. We were there to celebrate each other's success and the blessings that came to us as a couple. We were there to celebrate the birth and life of our children. We were there together to face the challenges, fears, and worries that are always a part of being parents. We were there together to share in their accomplishments and development into mature adults. And we were there to celebrate the transition to becoming grandparents.

We were there together to enjoy all the blessings and struggles of serving together in ministry, sharing in the joy of what God was doing and the anguish of seeing one we cared for and had invested in fail. We shared in the life, joys, and struggles of friends and coworkers.

We were there for each other to understand and help each other grow as we struggled to learn languages and cultures, several times. We shared in the frustrations and the achievements of each other. We could help each other see our mistakes and make the needed changes. We could help each see what had been gained in the process and how to build on it.

We were there for each other in all the good times and bad or rough times, the better or worse. But she has fulfilled her promise; the until death do us part clause has taken effect. I can no longer call on her to be with me for better or for worse. I am now alone to face the better or worse.

Even as I say that, that I may be on my own, I have our children, friends, and many coworkers who can help with going through the better and the worse with me. They can cry with me, celebrate with me, enjoy and suffer with me, but only to a certain extent. They cannot actually live with me and experience in real-time all that as my wife did.

To involve them will require a new type of commitment. It will require a new kind of sharing and living. It will also require understanding and accepting the fact that they can never do what my wife did and are not able to make that level of commitment to me. There is no "until death do us part" clause in those relationships. Do you understand what I am saying?

My wife was there for the richer or poorer part. Our finances were never such that we ever felt truly rich or truly poor. We never became millionaires, and we never became homeless and destitute. Well, in a sense we were homeless in that we always depended on someone else for a place to live. Still, we made it a home for us and our children and were never threatened with eviction or other frightening events that would leave us without a safe place.

But there were times when we struggled because finances were tight and times when life was good because there was enough finance to meet our needs and a little more. In all of that, we had each other to work through what was happening. We could bring our two perspectives together and make decisions that would help us deal with the richer or poorer.

A key part of this was knowing when someone needed something special or even necessary for work or life, something that would bring encouragement and a reminder that we were together in whatever was happening. Making sacrifices so each other could have a gift, a tool, or time to focus on one or the other. This allowed us to be rich even when we felt poor.

I no longer have her counsel related to how I can use what we have to help others. She was the more generous person, I was not so generous. Together we could find a balance that allowed us to help others appropriately.

Now her part of that process is fulfilled. I no longer can call on her for advice. I can no longer think about what she might need or want and what it will take to make it financially possible, and I no longer have someone doing the same for me.

I am in complete control of the finances. Again, there are those I can consult about big issues, such as investments and long-range financial planning. That has not changed since we used those sources as a couple. What has changed is the fact that I am shopping and living for one and not for two. I have no one to share what I buy with. I buy food for me, pay bills for me, and use my finances for me.

I do have the patterns that we set as a couple for many aspects of this, especially as relates to generosity toward others. For that I am thankful, and yet it is not the same. Doing it all on your own is not the same as doing it with someone else, not the same as sitting down and discussing what we need and how to handle it. It is a lonely feeling this richer or poorer as a solo.

And we promised that we would care for each other in sickness and health. And indeed, we did just that. I have had my share of challenging health situations: malaria more times than I can remember, an infection that almost cost me my foot, hepatitis, bowel infections, numerous wounds, and lacerations. She was always there. I was there for the morning sickness, her bout with dengue fever, and the years of cancer.

We were there together to enjoy times of health, which were more extensive than the times of sickness. Our health together allowed us to live in multiple countries and travel without reservation. We rarely had trouble with the food, the water, and life in other countries.

We were there together to take care of the kids when they were sick and to enjoy everything they did in their health. That included broken bones, lacerations, malaria, again, and all that comes with growing up. It included being present for as many sports activities, band concerts, and other events as possible while living the life of a missionary.

We were there for everything that is part of sickness and health, and now the contract is fulfilled. And I have become very aware of that reality as I have just had surgery to drain a nasty abscess. I was so grateful that a friend could spend a few days with me in my house. It was good to have someone near.

But it also highlighted what was missing. It made the fact that I was alone for two days with fever before the surgery a little more worrisome. And it heightened my awareness that I am alone. I have great friends who I can call. They can fill in some of the spaces when needed, but they cannot be with me 24/7. Even my family is too far away for that.

The vows have been fulfilled. I am no longer responsible for her. I don't have to deal with our life for better or for worse. I don't have to deal with what richer or poorer means for anyone but me. I am no longer responsible to care for her when she is sick or enjoy life together in health.

She is in heaven where everything is better, is wealthy beyond measure, and will never be concerned with her health again. And that means that I have fulfilled my vows to her. I did what I promised, and in all of life together, I did my part so both of us could arrive at the day of her death knowing we had fulfilled our vows to each other.

Those vows are done. and yet they are not. She may not be here to do her part, but our life together has created a pattern that will allow me to continue to live. Those vows were much more than dealing with life in the moment but about creating a way of thinking and living. Fulfilling those vows created the structures needed to follow God together, and that structure remains intact.

Keeping those vows has created a world I can live in and do more than just survive. They will provide all I need to grow and adapt as needed. Yes, the vows are fulfilled, my wife is gone. They gave us the strength to live our life together and now they have done something unexpected. They have created a way to live in the days ahead.

Until death do us part is not the end but a new beginning, if you are willing.

# Half-life, Half-time, Half Brain

The day my wife died I lost half my life. While I am using the concept of the half-life of radioactive material, it is not literally the same. Radioactive material slowly changes over time. As this process continues half of the radioactive material becomes non-radioactive. It becomes neutral. So slowly over time, half is lost. And then another half is lost over another equal period of time.

In the case of a marriage, this happens in an instant. Half of who I am disappeared. And no, a long-term sickness does not create a loss similar to the slow decay of radioactive material. There may appear to be some degradation in the relationship and status of life, but at the same time, other input and information is being gained. There may be loss in different areas, but there can be and often are gains to offset the losses. These gains are often not possible without the loss that can occur with long-term illness.

No, death is the sudden loss of half my life. In marriage, two become one; in death, the one becomes one-half. It is a strange math, but I live in its reality every day. And while I may remember some of what my life as one was before I went through the process of two becoming one, no matter how hard I try, I can't return to that level of one.

More interesting is that after the climatic shift to one-half, I sense there is a slow degradation of what is left. The speed of this will depend greatly on the profoundness of becoming one. I see this in the lives of others around me. I see it in the image of a husband, who twenty years after his wife's death, remains unmarried and has regular appointments to visit his wife's grave. I see it in a friend who less than four months after his wife's death is already remarried and to a person more than twenty years younger.

What does this mean? I am not totally sure, but I think in the one the degradation of the other half is much slower and provides great strength to continue living as half a person. This is possible, in my thinking, because the half that is left is not me or her but is a mix of both. I still have part of her in the half that remains. The more integrated our lives were, the oneness at a profound level, the easier it is to continue. I have half of us and not just a leftover me.

For the others, the issue is different. They cannot imagine being alone. They were dependent in so many ways on the marriage. They were one, but it was more built on dependency than on integration. This doesn't mean they didn't truly love each other, but losing half left them blind and lost. They may have actually lost more than half and so find themselves helpless, unable to draw on the oneness of the past to be able to live as a half, and so the disintegration proceeds more rapidly for them.

I watched my mother struggle with this. My father died, and she slowly began to fade. She was a people person, always busy, and slowly she began to withdraw and become lost. It was not until she met a new man and re-married that she regained her normal vibrancy and joy in life. She became involved in the world and people around her once again.

Sometimes the half-life actually can allow for growth and not decay. I am still trying to understand why this is happening. But I think it has to do with how well the couple integrated all aspects of their life into one united reality. How well they understood each other and challenged each other to excel in every way possible as individuals and as a one, and so explore life to its extreme in every situation. The one was not just a merging of life but allowed growth and development as the one. The one grew until when the death occurred the half that was left was so much more than the sum of the original two that became one.

Yes, I have lost half my life, but I am so much more than just half of what was. And I can grow because of what is left to me. I do not have to decay and become less. I can use what I have, the half that remains of the two who became integrated as one and then grew beyond that, into so much more.

The next concept is half-time. We are familiar with this term main-ly because of sports and the constant concept of taking a break to rest, recuperate, strategize, and refocus halfway through a game. Almost all sports provide this break (there are a few that have three periods and so go through this process twice). The key is that half of the time allotted to the event is past. Now it is time to take stock and consider what to do to win the contest. This involves maintaining a lead, adapting to changes the other team will make, overcoming a deficit, and replacing players if necessary. Often this break has amazing results in strengthening the team to maintain its lead and win or overcoming a deficit and winning.

For me, the idea of half time is somewhat like this. I have come to a break in life, a major pause, a time to evaluate where I am and what comes next. It means evaluating everything so that I can face the next time period and not lose.

The difference is that I have just lost half of my starting team. I have backup players, but it is not the same. It is not like in a real sports event where you may replace one or two players. I am replacing half of my team, and with people that need time to understand how I think and work. This was a process that took all of our married life to perfect, and even then, there were times when we had to admit that it wasn't working right and do some honest review and confession if needed.

Now I must replace her, the best player ever, with a group of people. It is a challenge because they all have their own lives and schedules. Instead of one person with one schedule and a clear understanding of how each other functions, thinks, and feels, it is multiple people with differences in each of those areas. Now instead of just walking to the next room to talk or consult, I will have to make plans and adapt to multiple schedules.

After thirty-nine years of marriage, you finish each other's thoughts or just know what the other person is thinking and feeling. If I can use the sport's concept here: when people play together enough, they begin to anticipate what the other team members will do. They say they click. Every coach looks for this, hopes for this, and when it happens, wonderful things are in the making. But change out a key person and the rhythm is affected; the anticipation doesn't happen, and the click is a dull thud.

Okay, do you get what I am saying? Half my team is gone, and I wonder if the click will ever come back. Over time, the others will replace her to some extent in some areas, but it will never be the same. And sometimes it just happens because all that she was is still a part of me. It is like when one player has an incredible game and lifts the whole team, but just for that game. But the click of becoming and being one cannot be duplicated or replaced. It may be simulated at some level, but never the same, and so half time has come. I will constantly be struggling, being creative in forming a new team, to find ways to live in the second half.

The last of my three things is half brain. The moment my wife died I lost half of my mental storage and acuity. Half of my memory disappeared in a moment. Ideas, images, memories, insights, all gone, never to be recovered.

Some might think that maybe I am referring to the idea that each person has a right and left half of their brain. The right half being the emotional creative side; the left being the analytical, structural side. I have reviewed this, and yes, the two halves of our brains have these kinds of specific functions. A lot of studies have been done to determine if in fact men and women have a dominant half. Scientifically this is not true. Both men and women utilize both halves of the brain. Men can be creative, and women can be analytical.

What I am talking about is like a hard drive crashing and before you can recover it half the data is gone; half the programs have been erased; half the processing power has been shorted out.

Let me explain. There would be times when we would be talking about things in the past and she or I would mention an event and the other person could not remember it at all. Then we would get into a discussion of events surrounding the person or place in question. Then there would be descriptions of the place, the time, and others present. Slowly the memory of the one would reawaken the other's memory, and then would come the aha moment of restored memory.

We remember things differently; we remember different things. We put the same memory in different contexts and perspectives. And in the moment of death, all that is gone. Half my memory of our history has been lost. Fortunately for me, I have a large collection of letters, photos, and documents to help restore some of this, but even then I know that as I look at a photo what I remember is less than what it would be if both of us looked at the photo together.

I have lost half of my capacity to process information. The saying, "Two heads are better than one," was never more accurate than when referring to a husband and wife processing information and sharing in the process of decision making. The context didn't matter: family, business, work issues, relationships, and on the list goes. We both gathered information that could be used in processing what was happening to put together a plan for what lay ahead or what must be done or even not done.

Now I don't have access to that. I do have a history section that I can use to help in thinking through what she might have said or thought. While it is useful, it is not current. I cannot simply restart or reboot. Critical files are gone and unrecoverable.

I have lost half of the ability to perceive the world around me. Before I had two sets of eyes and ears, and two of all the other senses. We complemented each other because of this. And over time, we learned how to interpret and benefit from the perspectives of each other. This meant we could create a more complete image of what was happening. This made it possible to do better at evaluating the meaning of events and relations and do a better job of decision making and responding to those around us.

Now it is gone. I have lost half of my brain, and I must learn to process anew the information around me and how to do better at dealing with what has been lost. It is difficult to have a person come to you and you don't remember them, but they remember you; they talk about a past event and you don't remember. More frustrating is the fact that you cannot consult the one person who could help you remember.

So, in many ways, I am half of who I used to be. It is a scary reality. How this is handled can result in frustration, a sense of inadequacy, even depression as one struggles to compensate. Here is where friends become critical. People who can fill some of the gaps, some of the memory lapses. People who have been, to some extent part of your life and willing to commit the time needed to help you move past the initial moments of loss.

It is much like a coach who had the best team the season before and half his team graduates. Depending on how well he has planned the next season, he will end up anywhere from a disaster to very hopeful. For me, the issue is, will I invest in those around me so that they can help with any of the issues above? Their ability will depend on how open I am to them and how well I communicate what I need in any given moment or situation. It will also be affected by how much I live in a past that no longer exists and how well I move into and adapt to the new future of the next half.

# It Is Still Mourning

While I was visiting a friend, he looked at me and then commented to those around him that I was still in mourning. It had been seven months since my wife died, and I wondered what he meant by that. Now, over a year later, I am just beginning to understand.

While some cultures define what is considered an appropriate time of mourning, the time for being dressed in the clothing related to mourning; the rituals and rites to be completed in the time of mourning, and so on – others don't. The time of mourning can be anywhere from a few months to years. It is also often determined by your relation to the one who has died. It is shorter for those not as close, usually a friend or non-family members. For those with a closer relation, the period of mourning will be longer. The longest being for the loss of a spouse.

In many of these, the time is established and must be completed before the remaining spouse is free to participate in the normal flow of life around them. Any attempt to avoid this or shorten it is seen as an affront to the one who has died and a sign of disrespect. This will impact negatively not only the person in mourning and their acceptance in the culture but also can create issues for their family.

So how does that affect me and my culture? In my situation, there is no specific time that has been set for what would be an acceptable period of mourning. I sense that it is at least a year and maybe more. It all depends on the nature of the relationship between the one who has died and the individual who is still living. In this case, I am focusing mainly on the death of a spouse.

I have seen people who cannot handle the impact of this loss nor deal with all that happens and is part of the mourning process. I know a person who struggled deeply with the loneliness and other issues and remarried in less than six months. They did not consult the family, and the person they married is more than twenty years younger. This decision has created a great deal of tension in the family. Questions arise like: How could you do this and show such lack of honor and respect for our mother, grandmother, etc? How could you do this without consulting us or considering our feelings? How could you be so insensitive to us and the rest of the family?

It becomes obvious that this person has not handled the process and the impact of loss and mourning well. To avoid the emotions and stress the person filled the emptiness before dealing with it properly, at least in the eyes of the family and others. The truth is that mourning is not a solo event and involves others. That means how I handle mourning can be a source of blessing or distress to others. In this case, I am not talking about my need for the help of others in processing all that is helping. I am talking about how my willingness to accept the loss, accept the help of others, and so move through all the pain to a place of healthy emotion and proper response to my loss allows others to process this loss.

I have also seen another strange event. Even before the spouse's death, the wife was trying to find a new wife for her husband. To me, this is truly strange. The reasoning behind this had to do with how long the wife had been sick, ten years with colon cancer, and decades with bipolar disorder. No matter what we think of the action of the wife, it allowed her husband to handle the mourning process. He remarried within six months of her death. I have talked with a few family members and though they questioned what was happening; they kept an open mind to this process. They knew the history, had seen the struggle over the years. They also saw the positive impact and freedom that came with the new marriage and how the permission to remarry allowed him to process the loss and open the door to a new life and restoration of joy in his life.

The flip side of this is the person who never seems to stop mourning. They never remarry. They never let others into their life. So potent is their morning that ten, twenty, thirty, and more years may have passed, and they are still mourning. Life goes on, but it is clearly affected, colored, and influenced by the loss. The phrase, *I remember when . . .* has a central focus in most if not all of their conversations. When people try to suggest it is time to move on, this person becomes incensed at the idea and the disrespect toward the one who has died.

This person never puts anything of their spouse away, never gets rid of anything. The closets, drawers, and spaces still contain clothing, articles, and other items as a constant reminder of the person. They are constantly visiting the grave site or special places to remember and honor their spouse. There is no consideration, no admittance of the possibility of ever remarrying, because in their mind that would be wrong.

In the end, life is under control of the past with no room for a future that does not give a large space to the one that was lost. This keeps people at a distance, emotionally and physically. People can only handle so much of this type of mourning before it becomes easier to avoid being with the person in such a level of mourning. Being together is barely tolerated and limited to only what is necessary to avoid being attacked for being insensitive and creating isolation and rejection. This is the perspective of the person in this type of mourning. There is no concept that it is not about the person but about their attitude and constant mourning and insistence that everyone who comes into their circle of contact must share in this.

Those are the two extremes. I am somewhere in the middle. I know that whatever is happening in my life means I am still in this process. In fact, in some ways, the loss has been more intense lately. It may have to do with the fact that last month was the anniversary of her death. It may be that I am also dealing with a number of critical things in my life, and she is not here to help me in dealing with these issues – issues of health, future work, when to retire, and so on.

Yet, it may have nothing to do with any of this. Loss is a moving target as I have stated earlier. You never know what will trigger the emotions of loss and remind you of what you no longer have. This is the impact and reality of what mourning is. What has been a surprise is the depth of those emotions even after a year. I have learned to order my days to deal with what my wife cared for. I have learned to lean on a few others as needed. I have asked others to help in key areas because she is not available to help me.

What is interesting is that though I have done fairly well at making the adjustments, there are two things that I have noticed. One, there are areas where there is no adaptation, change, or investment in the new that will ever replace what has been lost. At least for now. Maybe somehow in the future, but I can't see that future, or if I began to see it, it is shrouded in what I see as impossible and unreal. I am still too much caught up in mourning to see this. Two, in the areas where I have made the adjustments, changes, and inclusion of others, in those areas where it is possible, they rise up and remind me of what is no longer accessible to me. Not always, just often enough to heighten my senses and remind me I am still in the period of mourning.

I wish I could say how long this will last. I can't. But I am beginning to understand a comment of one of my children of how the sense of loss had grown and not diminished. For that child, the mourning was deep and intense, and it will take time and patience for it to soften and for there to be a peace about what has been lost. And I am beginning to understand how for some the mourning, or aspects of it, can last for years, even decades. The key issue is to embrace this reality but not let it dominate and entomb me in the past, making it impossible to live in the present and move to the future.

I have to learn when it is appropriate to talk about and discuss how life was with my wife. There are times when it is appropriate and beneficial, and to learn when it is not appropriate. Like trying to include a reference to her in every comment and conversation no matter what the topic may be. This will prevent me from properly handling the process of mourning and will drive away those who come in contact with me, both those close and those unconnected to her life and death.

For some, the mourning never starts or is interrupted and avoided. They deny the emotion and try to live as if the loss had no effect on their life. This is unwise and is a dangerous way to live. They try to forget the past and create a future without the pain of loss.

For some, the mourning never ends. Every day is a day of loss, and it goes on for years. I am still trying to understand what this means, but in some ways this person never moves into the future. They never allow themselves to move on and find life after loss. I can think of a few reasons for this, but the reason is not the issue. The issue is they allow themselves to avoid the future and spend a great deal of effort to maintain their pain and loss in the present

But, in some way, both ideas and responses are necessary. If we don't move beyond the mourning at some point, we will be trapped in a false, past existence. If we don't deal with the mourning, we will be trapped in a present existence just as false and unreal. Both are forms of denial and we must avoid both.

*It is still mourning.* Strange phrase but so true. How I feel and live is still mourning. My need is to understand its truth and incorporate it into my life so that I can live and benefit from the past and loss, so as to create a future that is healthy and whole. How this will all happen is yet to be determined. I can make it torturous or embrace the adventure that it may provide – an adventure to a blended life of the past, present, and a possible future – all because I mourned in a way that brought honor to my wife and all she represents in me and opened the door to grow and live.

# Four Layers of Loss

There is a scripture that talks about the greatest commandment. Briefly, we are to love the Lord our God with all our heart, mind, soul, and strength. The second is to love your neighbor as yourself (Mk 12:29–30). These are two powerful statements, and at first glance, they would appear very different. Our love for God is all-encompassing, and our love for ourselves is something less. But how do you love yourself? Do you not focus on the same areas? Do you not want to make sure you are mentally, emotionally, spiritually, and physically committed to doing the best possible job of loving who you are and caring for yourself?

We expend a great deal of energy in training our minds. We spend a great deal of energy on being emotionally healthy. We make sure that our soul is cared for, and we have answers for the great questions and issues of life. And we most definitely spend a lot of time and money on the care of our physical being to be sure we have the strength to do all that we want to do.

And that is how we are to love our neighbor.

Now for the key issue related to grief: Where does one's spouse fit in this commitment of my total being to God, and in the same way, a commitment that makes it possible for me and my neighbor to know the fullness of love? This is something that is only possible if we first truly love God as described above. Then once I understand this, what have I lost now that my wife has died?

The first part is somewhat obvious. Even so, we do not do all that we should do to make it a reality. And it is a two-sided concept. It involves a mix of how I treat me, which then becomes how I treat my spouse. Remember, in marriage, the two become one. How I treat me, how I love me in each area, results in a layer of the process of how I treat my wife.

Here is an extreme example. If I am careless and constantly putting myself at risk with little regard to the consequences, then I will create stress and worry in my wife. If I am careless in my treatment of others, then this will impact how others treat my wife and, in turn, her perception of whether or not I care about how my behavior affects her.

We could do this for each of the areas – how well I work at developing my mind and skills, how careful I am about dealing with emotions and being honest, how much time I invest in spiritual matters, and how and what I invest in caring for my physical being or strength as is mentioned in the scripture.

But remember marriage is a two-way street. Even as my wife is affected by what I do, I am affected by what is happening in her life. The beauty of this is that now two people are working for the same goal, a marriage that can be fully committed in love to God. This is not always true, but when it is, God can do some unique and special things in and through this marriage of one being. That is when there is unity in heart, mind, soul, and body. And when there is this kind of unity, it is wondrous.

When two people have the love of God as their center, then life is blessed.

But now to the point of this book, grief, the loss of that partner in working towards truly loving God with all one's heart, mind, soul, and strength. What is lost in death?

First, there is something that is not lost. All that has been learned and done is still a part of me. I am especially blessed because in many areas of life we were united. Not perfectly. We are humans after all, and perfection, while our goal, is never quite possible. But again, that is not the focus of this. I am not looking at all that has been but at how the death of my wife has affected me and what I have lost.

Let me start with the last item and work backward through the list.

I have lost her body or strength. I want to divide this into two aspects, physical contact and physical presence. The first is physical presence. Her presence brought strength to me. We hosted people together; we sought to use our strength as a couple to encourage others. The work was always easier because there were two of us to share the tasks. Even when others were involved, the presence of each other created strength to deal with issues and carry out the work involved. In fact, we didn't have to be physically present to draw on each other's strengths. We knew that each other was working to help carry out whatever task, job, or goal that had been set.

In some ways, I can still draw on this. I know what we desired to do and how each of us would have contributed to accomplishing the work. We had desired to travel and teach. Now she is gone, and when I travel, I will do so alone, but still able to draw on the knowledge that if she were there, she would give her all to make sure our goals and plans were a success.

In the same way, I have found myself stepping in to complete some goals and plans she had. It has not been easy because my role was to help her carry them out and not necessarily do the actual work. I was there to assist her. Now I am the one doing the work and only can imagine what it would be like if she were present so I could draw on her physical presence.

The farther I am from the date of her death, the more challenging this becomes. It is harder because I often have to do the work alone. Even when others are there to help, it is not the same. I still have the memory of her strength to draw on, but I can no longer draw on her physical presence, on her to share in the work. I have lost my workmate and her strength.

Keep in mind, I am not just talking about physical strength. There is emotional strength as well, but experienced and known in the context of physical presence. Which brings us to the second aspect of strength: physical contact.

In life, we develop rituals and patterns of contact. Each couple has their way to hold hands, to hug, to kiss, to caress each other. This ranges from what happens in public to what happens in the privacy of the bedroom.

Each of these areas allows us to draw strength from each other. It is amazing how powerful a peck on the cheek or the squeeze of one's hand in a certain way, as well as the touch on the shoulder, a hug, oh there are so many ways we touch each other. Each one brings, joy, peace, comfort, and more. And each of these brings strength.

How we lay beside each other, sit beside each other, and make contact in so many different ways all bring with them a special reality. I am not alone; I can draw on the strength of another. In a healthy marriage, we use these points of physical contact to strengthen each other, lighten the load of each other, soften the pain we feel, and on the list goes.

But now those touches of physical contact are gone. I sit down and there is no one beside me; I lay down and there is no one beside me. I reach out my hand, but there is no hand reaching out to me. You may say other people can do this. Others who can give me a hug, hold my hand, but it never carries the same message, nor can it ever be done with the same level of intimacy and understanding. But without those substitutes, the loss of strength through physical contact could easily become unbearable. The memory of those things is wonderful, but it will never equal a real physical touch. I am blessed because of all I have had, and I feel deeply what I have lost.

There is one other aspect. It is not just her touch that is gone. It is also the fact that I cannot reach out and touch her. It is hard to explain what it means to be able to touch someone and bring them comfort, confidence, and so much more, just because you held their hand, hugged them, lay next to them with no word being said.

Yes, I can do this for others. I have done so and will continue to do so. And I will draw on all that I have exchanged with my wife to fill those actions with more strength than I have in myself alone. And for those people, there will be great power in such physical contact because they see both my wife and I in it. But for me, it sometimes is, all too often, a reminder of what I have lost.

I have lost the power of her physical touch, to lift my spirits, to encourage me, to just let me know I am not alone, there is someone on whose strength I can draw. I have lost the joy of doing the same for her.

I have lost this.

The next layer is my soul. Let me very specific as to what this means. This is what makes me, me. It is who I am as a person: my personality, my focus, everything that identifies me as unique from others. I have unique strengths, unique attitudes, and unique experiences. Unique is the keyword.

In marriage, we begin the blending of two such souls. Two people that are unique, who have a goal, combine their uniqueness in the creation of a blended soul. Two people who have chosen, not to give up who they are, but use all of who they are to become one with another person.

If they are successful, the two people still exist but in harmony. It would be like a composer who writes a symphony with two key melodies that step by step become blended into one without losing a single note in the process. The first one rises, while the other is the harmony, then the other grows in prominence while supported by the first, and at times the two become so perfectly blended they create a unique melody that encompasses both and soars. It soars because they carry each other farther than they could go alone.

Now that is gone. Now all that is left is a recording. And while the recording is great and at times it almost, but only almost, sounds the same, it can't because recordings are just that. They can't match what happens in real time. They can't match what one experiences when present for the actual performance. You are the melody, and all the emotion and energy of the composer; and all the musicians are part of all that makes up your soul.

Now it is one person trying to sing both parts of a duet. It can't happen. And even if you find someone to sing with you, it is never the same as the original. Not because it can't be better, but it will never have the same soul content.

That is what I have lost. Half my soul, half the music, and in many ways so much more. My identity was intricately woven together with hers.

A very clear example of this is a tapestry. We brought our own colors and patterns to the loom, and they were woven into a wondrous and beautiful tapestry. I still have what has been created, but now it is left undone and will be impossible for me to duplicate or finish what has been done up until now. Not because I don't desire to do so, or don't remember the identity of the soul of my wife. It is because it will be based on memory and not reality. It is a solo work and not a joint work where each of us continues to grow and develop more skill and unity in the work. Now it is just me, or actually me and her up to a point, and then just me. Now I feel lost.

I had my individual identity, then spent a lifetime developing a new soul, a conjoined soul that would honor God. Now I have been separated and must depend on myself to continue something that required two people to accomplish.

I have lost half of my soul, and so in a real way, a portion of my ability to continue to grow and develop. It will require developing new skills and understanding, learning how to remember what I have gained and allowing others to have input into the continued development of the tapestry.

One last word here: It is a tapestry that tells a story. It can be continued. Except it will be clear where the story changed and the fact that a key contributor is now gone, and so the story changes shape and has lost a soul, a key actor.

The next is mind. You know the old saying, two heads are better than one. It is so true. Two minds bring to every decision, every experience, two perspectives. Two minds always can see more than one.

And then there is the other one, two minds that think alike. This is not so much that they have become duplicates of each other but that they know how each other thinks. People who have been married complete each other's sentences, communicate with a nod, a glance, a look. It is not that they have become one mind, but they have developed an understanding of each other's ideas, preferences, and potential.

It also means there is more room and time for more important matters. You are not always starting at the beginning and establishing the foundations for the conversation. That has already been established and allows you to quickly make many decisions because you already know what the other is thinking and what needs to be done. It also makes handling more complicated situations simpler.

Geometry provides a great example. You start by learning the basic rules and laws. Once they are learned, then you apply them to more complex problems and establish more critical guidelines and laws. Step-by-step foundations are laid to solve more and more complex problems. The key is that you don't have to go back and reestablish the foundational principles to move forward. It goes like this: Given this and this, then this is possible. And on it goes. Every time these two minds work together, they have a greater understanding and a greater capacity to handle more and more.

My wife was my best editor. She was excellent regarding knowledge of grammar, spelling, and phrasing. But even more importantly, she knew how I thought and processed information. And that knowledge helped me do a better job of writing and communicating. I knew her ability and could help her see beyond the evident to more possibilities. She knew how my mind worked and how I could see things from many angles.

And in our service to the Lord, it worked the same way. We had our own skills and abilities but had a oneness of mind. We knew why we were serving, and how to help each other do the best job possible. We had gathered more and more knowledge that we could use to expand the horizon of understanding and capacity to learn from each and then teach others what we had learned. We saw just how wonderful this was as we worked together on a cross-cultural training program. Our understanding of each other's minds and knowledge became a valuable tool as we worked together to develop a tool to help train others to live in another culture.

But that is gone. I still have much I can draw on. All that I learned from working together and sharing in each other's goals, knowledge, and focus is still mine. But that is never the same as her actually being there to work with. I had to finish the final revision of that material. We had spent hours working on this and had almost finished. As I worked on the final part, which was an area where she had great input, I felt the loss. All the comments and ideas she would have contributed to that last section were no longer accessible. I had lost a part of my mind; now I only had access to half of what we knew together.

As I continue to write, I no longer can benefit from her knowledge of me, how I think, and our experiences together. It is all gone. It is all lost.

The last item is heart. There is a saying that involves two hearts beating as one. Two hearts sharing the same joys, same success, same desires. Two hearts deeply entwined, knowing each other's strengths, and weaknesses. Two hearts helping each other to survive, live, to grow in times of sorrow and struggle.

We became one heart. We lived for each other and through each other. We didn't need to be reminded of our marriage vows. Love, honor, and cherish, in sickness, and health, for richer or poorer, until death do us part. Those vows faded into the background of what love means and are only a dim reflection of what it means to have one heart.

You are the richest person in the world because there is another heart beating in tune with you. That is true wealth. A wealth that cannot be purchased or created. It only becomes real as your heart and your emotions become entwined with another. When every joy, every struggle, every success, every failure becomes yours as a couple.

And the poor part. Well, though many people think of that as one's economic state, and that is a factor: poor is about our heart as well. It is about when I feel empty and lost; I know there is one near to help me recover. Not to recover lost goods or materials, but to recover who I am because they have within them part of my heart and they guard it against all storms, against all ruin.

So even when we have lost material goods, even family and friends, and in the world's eyes may appear poor, we still have wealth unimaginable. We have each other's hearts.

The sickness and health are the same. Because we are committed to each other and have hearts beating as one, hearts ready to sacrifice all for the other, we have an incredible health. It may not be physical health; our bodies may be falling into decay by reason of disease or age. It doesn't matter; we have one heart, a heart that beats for each other and gives strength no matter the condition of the body.

That means you are the healthiest person because there is another heart beating with you that you can draw strength from.

But I have lost all of that. Again, while it is true that I can draw on all the experience of the past to continue the journey and guide me in both aspects of the good and bad, I no longer have that person at my side to share in all the emotions, to share in all the current hopes and desires. That can no longer exist because it was based on two hearts beating as one.

And while people will say I have been a faithful husband and truly lived out the reality of those vows, that is all past. Death has severed those bonds and left me somewhat adrift. I have lost my strength. I have lost my soul. I have lost my mind. I have lost my heart.

It is painful, and I am still working on understanding how to live in my new condition. I am thankful for all that I still have, all the time together, all the experience shared, all the love lived. And it is that storehouse of our life together that helps me continue to move forward, to continue to be open to all that lies before. But there remains the reality that I have lost much that I will never be able to restore or duplicate.

I am a blessed man. And I know the beauty and blessing of what I have lost.

# The Pendulum

Sometimes it is necessary to allow time to pass before some aspects of grief become clear. It has now been a year and a half since my wife died, and I am learning more about my grief and how it can affect me in both expected and unexpected ways. It would be so nice if grief were simple and easily understood, but it is an incredibly complex emotion.

There are some things that are predictable. Then there are others that are not. You don't realize what is happening until you find yourself enveloped in situations and times that want to derail the smooth flow of emotions.

That means the factors that become part of this reality are also numerous and complex. To better explain this, the concept of a pendulum came to mind.

In previous reflections, many of these have been mentioned. Events that are repetitive, like birthdays, anniversaries and other personal dates, like the first date, the day one proposes, the dates of birth of children, and therein lies part of the issue. The list can go on and on.

Why? Because each of us can make a list of dates or events that become unique and special to us in our marriage. And this list reflects the marriage and life lived. For me, a special day would be when we arrived in Sierra Leone or when Nancy and I received the diagnosis of her cancer. And as you think through this, you will begin to realize you have your own list that uniquely reflects your life as a couple.

Here is where things get complicated. We don't apply the same value or weight to each of these moments in our life and history. That means one year we may be very focused on an event because of what is happening in our life at that moment, and the next we may hardly remember it. In another situation, two events may occur close to each other and don't simply add but multiply their effect on us.

So why the idea of a pendulum? First, it reflects the flow of normal events that repeat themselves every year. Those key events that everyone is aware of, and as a result, there is a greater likelihood that they will be brought to mind and create a response. You expect it because, like the pendulum and its movement, it is predictable. And as the pendulum moves, its weight varies. At the bottom of its swing, it is at its highest velocity and weight. And when it reaches its highest point in the swing, it is at its lowest velocity and weight. If you want, I can explain the physics involved, but that would be way over the top. Trust me, what I have said is correct.

Actually, it is not hard to explain. Think of a roller coaster. As it comes to the bottom you feel the force as you hit the bottom of a curve. And in reverse, as you hit the top of a curve you feel a sort of weightlessness.

But what has not changed is the mass of the pendulum. This remains the same. Grief is grief. What shifts is how we experience it. There are times when it feels light and almost undetectable. Then there are times when it is heavy and very evident. And we can predict to a great degree when both occur. Another factor is if there is an outside force being applied to maintain the movement. Like a spring in a clock, which when wound keeps the pendulum swinging at its maximum. Remove the spring, and over time the pendulum will slow and stop.

The spring in grief is the comments and actions of others reminding us of those events and who is missing. They choose not to forget and so act as a spring to keep the pendulum moving in our lives and theirs. We do the same thing as well. We choose to remember, to honor, to encourage the memories of those key events. We review photos, we talk about the past, and we do what is needed to keep the pendulum in movement, and we are pleased when others help us do so.

We do this for many reasons. A key one is to honor the one that is gone. Another would be to keep alive the work or ministry they have done. A negative one would be to avoid guilt. Guilt that comes by not doing something, which results in the fear that we are committing an error, even sinning against them, if we don't keep the pendulum swinging, that somehow, we no longer value who the person was in our life.

Another is to avoid negative comments from others. How can you not remember her birthday, your anniversary, or the day she died? Guilt is a powerful motivator to keep the pendulum swinging. Both internal, my fear of feeling guilty for not helping the pendulum swing, and external, not responding to the need of others to keep the pendulum swinging.

This process will continue for years and cause a person to evaluate each year how much force to continue to apply to the pendulum. How long the pendulum continues to swing will depend on the person and those close to the person. For some, the pendulum will continue to be in motion until they die. For some, less time. To be honest, the pendulum will never stop swinging because there will always be key dates that will remind one of the loss, and once again keep the pendulum in motion.

I have seen parents talking about a child who died at birth forty or more years after the event. That keeps the pendulum in motion. Another continues to place flowers on the grave of their spouse ten, twenty, and more years after their death. In fact, they continue to do so until they die. But it may not stop there because the children may keep this pendulum moving with their actions. The action may not be taken every year, but often enough for the pendulum of grief to remain in motion.

What I have explained is the basic concept of a pendulum and its movement. But the pendulum of grief is more complex than what one observes when watching a grandfather clock or other clock that depends on a pendulum for keeping time. This pendulum relates to keeping memories alive, keeping the grief evident in their life.

The mathematical equations for the motion of a pendulum are not simple, but at the same time not overly complex. But the pendulum of grief has more factors affecting it than the basic x and y coordinates that control the swing of the pendulum; x and y define what happens in a specific line and place. To fully understand the pendulum of grief, we need to add three more factors, a z coordinate, a coordinate for time, and another for special circumstances.

Grief is not restricted to swinging in a specific arc defined by a specific path. It can sway side to side as it swings. This is the z coordinate and represents all the unique events and memories that are part of the life of grief. These events are often not consistent in how they impact the movement. They also can be cumulative. More than one can come into play and make the sway more pronounced. And what is causing the sway today may not be what causes the sway tomorrow.

How do I explain this? This can be triggered by the arrival of a person who you haven't seen since your wife died; it could be caused by attending an event for the first time without your wife. And the impact is then multiplied because both events happened at the same time. Then it is followed by returning home from the event and entering an empty house without your wife. Three things that are not part of the regular cycle of events have come together to create a sway in the movement of the pendulum of your grief. And to complicate it more, it can happen in conjunction with the normal expected events of grief. Those that are part of the normal swing but are now complicated by the z, time, and special circumstance coordinates.

If you are not prepared for this, then the sway can potentially cause too much sway and so hit the case in which the pendulum swings, or even hit with enough force to cause the case to fall over. At least that is a fear we have. What is needed is a dampener. Something to moderate the impact of this possibility.

Let me explain this a little more. Think of a washing machine. It has its normal agitator mode for washing. Then it has a spin mode. I have noted that the different materials being washed, or quantity of materials being washed, can affect the spin mode. Most of the time the clothes spread evenly and the drum spins with no wobble. But at other times because of the nature of the contents of the laundry, it is unbalanced. As it picks up speed, you can hear the fact that it is out of balance and wobbling; it bangs.

Sometimes it overcomes this as the water is drained out. Then there are times when that is not enough. Many machines have a failsafe that shuts the spin cycle down and allows the wash to resettle, and then the spin restarts. On some occasions, it is not enough, and the machine just keeps on stopping and starting. At that point, it becomes necessary to open the machine and manually relocate some of the laundry.

Without this resetting, the machine can be damaged by the wobble in the load. In the same way, if the clock with a swaying pendulum is not anchored and the issue causing this sway is not identified and properly dealt with, then damage is possible and almost inevitable.

Actually, I find myself in the midst of one of these wobbles, and it is proving to be fairly severe. This time of year is a time when the pendulum of my grief hits one of the periods when it is at its heaviest point in the swing. Within a short period of four weeks, I will encounter four events, her birthday, Mother's Day (where I currently live it is held on December 8), our anniversary, and Christmas.

All normal, but because they are so close together, more intense. Additionally, I have just returned from an event that for the past twelve years my wife attended with me, and I met many people for whom it was the first time to express their grief and sense of loss. And to further intensify the situation, I have a visitor coming. This visitor has been a very close friend for the last nineteen years. The last time I saw him, my wife was alive. He is coming to join me in a time of ministry. But I already know that it will also be a time of remembering and talking about the past. Again, normal, but the combination of all these at the same time has created a wobble in my emotions.

You cannot avoid these events. And you cannot predict how much $z$ will be applied, how much the time and circumstances will affect your grief. Remember, too, this is not just cumulative in nature, but multiplied.

The most important way to deal with this is by being aware of the kinds of events that trigger the wobble in your grief. Not the regular events, but other situations or conditions.

I have learned a few:

1. Coming home after a trip. My wife usually picked me up at the airport, and then we came home together. Now it is a friend, and I come home to an empty house. It took me a few trips to realize what was happening the first days after returning. I still feel the impact of this, but now I am aware and can better face this reality.

2. We spent time together reviewing my trips, our plans, and other aspects of life as well as what she had been doing. Now I have no one to do this with. Friends who are willing to listen help, but they cannot replace at any level having a person ready to talk 24/7. That means I have to be more conscious about finding people to share with.

3. My wife was my editor. So, every time I finish a new chapter in a writing project, I feel this loss. So far, I have not been able to find any replacement for this aspect of our life together, and it creates a unique wobble in my pendulum. I have four people who have agreed to help, but it is not the same. They cannot dedicate the same amount of time and energy to this as my wife did. Further, they cannot sit down with me and go over their recommendations in the same way. My wife came into my office, sat down on my lap, and then we reviewed her editing. That is not going to happen with those who have agreed to help me. In fact, it is unlikely that I will have face-to-face conversations with them because of where everyone lives.

I can think of more, but this is enough. Each of us will discover that there are areas of our life that are unique, and when those areas overlap each other or occur in the context of the regular cycle of grief, then the pendulum can begin to wobble in its path; and that is unsettling.

Do I have solutions? A few, but they are my solutions or contingencies that I can use and depend on.

1. People who are praying for you and really do want to know how

you are doing. These people don't need details. They just are willing to pray and listen as needed.

2. Prayer and time alone with God. If you have a solid relationship with God, then you have access to incredible resources and comfort.
3. Key friends that you can share in detail with. These are not just any friend. They are the ones that will walk the extra mile with you and learn what it means to walk in your shoes. They may not understand exactly what you are dealing with but are capable of creating a safe place based on their own experiences and understanding of the need for someone to just be there.
4. Escape is always an option. This is not about running away and never turning back. This is about finding space to let things settle. It is about allowing yourself time to deal with the wobble; a time to reduce the number of events in play and allow you to gain some control of them; a time to identify what is causing the wobble and, in that recognition, diminish its effect.

And so, the pendulum is swinging. My grief ebbs and flows as it swings up and down. At times other factors become involved, and the pendulum wobbles. When that happens, I feel unsettled. I hope the anchors used to hold the clock in place will be adequate and strong enough to allow me to deal with the wobble before it becomes dangerous. I also hope the guides that have been installed to keep the pendulum in its proper track will do so without damaging the pendulum.

I have just added a new concept to all of this by talking about anchors and guides. These have to do with our relationship with God, friends, and family. They have to do with our openness about what is happening and allowing others inside to help us process our grief and to make sure we are responding appropriately to our grief.

As much as some people may think it is true, that grief is a private emotion; that is false. Locking it up inside will eventually create fallout in your life and affect others. And, to be honest, grief is a group event or reality. You are not the only one dealing with the loss. Whatever that loss is, it affects more than just you, and so bottling it up and hiding it away will be detrimental to all of those dealing with the grief tied to the loss that is shared in common.

They help keep the pendulum of grief moving. They also create the sway, and they are a big part of the factors of time and circumstance. Finally, they are also those who help provide the anchors and guides needed to control that sway.

Grief is a pendulum, and the best way to keep its motion correct and balanced is to understand that reality and how others are critical to keeping your personal pendulum in balance so that all of those suffering from this loss can do the same.

# Well Digging

Have you ever dug a well? Probably not. I have made the attempt on two occasions. Neither of them was very successful. In the first, I hit a big rock that protruded out of the side of the well. I tried to get around it, tried to break it, but it won. I had the joyous task of having to fill the hole, about twenty feet deep, to make sure no one fell in it.

The second was not so deep, and I did hit water, but again I hit a rock. Try as I might, with the tools available, I could not break through. At least I did hit water, and because I dug this well in the dry season, I knew that when the rains started, the water table would rise, and there would be water. I had hoped to get deep enough so we could water a nursery full of palm trees we wanted to plant when the rains started again. While it didn't supply water at that time, it did make getting water easier once the rains came. The bible school students were happy that we had dug the well because it was closer to the dorms and was much cleaner than other sources of water.

So why am I telling you this? In our lives, we work at developing relationships. They become wells that we hope will supply us with needed resources in our lives. We also hope that they will be deep enough to reach what is needed with sufficient access to meet the needs that will come. These are family relationships, friendships, student/teacher relations, and others. Together we work at digging into life with the purpose of developing a well that will provide key resources when needed.

When searching for a future marriage partner, we do the same thing. As we meet and date others, we are in a way digging a well to find out what is there and if we can work together to create a well of resources. Sometimes the relationships are brief. The ground is too hard, there are obstacles, and we just don't know how to work/live together. Even if we do reach deep enough, we may discover it has limitations and will not be adequate when the time comes to provide what is needed to sustain the relationship to face the challenges of life.

It is hoped that we see this before we commit ourselves to that relationship. Also, that we agree with what is seen. Sometimes one person thinks they see more than is really there and pushes the relationship forward even though there are insufficient resources in the relationship. This may be a result of being desperate to be married, not be alone, and other similar desires, which means the well will never be properly dug or deep enough to even begin the marriage. It will take a major shift in thinking for that couple to invest what is needed to finish digging until they gain access to those resources. If they don't, the marriage may not last; and if it does, it will be filled with strife and more.

A strong marriage understands this, and there is a willingness of both to go deep enough into the process of developing the well that is their life as one. As they work together, it becomes clear that the obstacles can be overcome, and an adequate depth can be reached for both people to believe and know they will have access to what is needed. The goal is to reach the water table or an underground spring so there will always be resources available as long as it is maintained correctly.

Now I need to correct a possible error in the perception of what is happening here. I am not talking about each person digging a well in the life of another person. That does not work. The old way of digging a well always works best if there are two people. One is digging at the bottom and the other above has a rope and bucket to draw the dirt out, and later lower stones and mortar to line the well. While it is possible for a person to dig a well, it is incredibly difficult and slow. Imagine having to descend into the well, fill the bucket, then ascend to raise the bucket and lower it once again into the well. Then imagine repeating this process over and over. It is exhausting work for two. For one person, more than doubly so.

Relationship development is the same. Two people digging a well. Two people committed to sharing and growing in the process. Two people seeking a resource that will bring benefit to them both. Two people helping each other grow strong and learn to trust each other.

There's one last thing: this well is the project of a lifetime. Why? The dating and pre-wedding time is to discover if a well can be dug, if these two people can become one and succeed. The early years are the time when the well is deepened and improved and lined. As life moves forward and others become part of one's life, children, friends, coworkers, etc., the focus is on maintaining the well and making sure there are adequate resources for all of life. Wells dug in this way need to be lined with stone or brick, cleaned, deepened from time to time. The equipment used to draw from the well also needs care and maintenance. An excellent well provides physical, emotional, and spiritual resources. It is about tapping into each other's strengths, emotions, and relationships with God. You never stop caring for the well.

I have taken a fair bit of time to explain the concept of a well. I have done so because it creates a powerful image of marriage and what happens as two people become one and work together to develop a relationship that will provide what they need and to provide for those who will become part of their lives at different stages. It is about them working together to create access to a fountain of resources that is always adequate to meet whatever happens in their life.

A day will come when one of the partners in this well-digging dies. The "until death do us part" will come. It is inevitable. The one is gone but the well is still there. All that they have built will remain. I am learning that I do not stop being married to my wife even though she has died. I have found that I cannot separate her from me. That would be a dangerous action. And as I allow this reality to settle in my heart and my mind, I find that the well we dug together, all the resources we discovered, is still there for me to access.

If we have done our work properly, the well will need little maintenance and I will benefit from all that has been done for years to come. Of course, it will not be the same. It can't be. She is gone. I cannot have that face-to-face conversation. I cannot hold her hand. But I can remember and allow it to lift me and help me when I am struggling. I can remember how we handled this and that and use that knowledge to handle what happens in the future.

And with my spouse's death, I do not have as much of the resource of the well available at any moment. There is only one of us drawing from the well. I can see this fact in many different ways. I cannot ask her to cook, to edit my latest material, and so on. That can be frustrating, but what I can draw on is her way of encouraging me to live, to care about others, and to keep writing. The work we did together continues, and I depend on what she did to be able to continue forward with that ministry.

I am also learning about how to care for this well without her. We raised three children; two are married, and there are now three grandchildren. They can help in different ways to keep the well in working order. They benefited from its resources for years and in different ways. They help provide some of the energy needed to keep the well in good shape. We also developed relationships at many levels, personal and professional. I am learning that many of these people are willing to help fill the place of my wife. It is not at the same level, but it helps.

The challenge here is learning how to involve others in maintaining this well we dug together and keep it in good condition so that all those who benefited from it will be able to continue to do so. And if I may be a little selfish, so that I can continue to enjoy all we created in our marriage even now that she is gone.

Two dangers can arise in this process. We can turn this into a wanting well, always wanting others to fill the gap left by the one who has died. They can't, but we want this to happen. Let me explain. My wife and I lived together. I am stating the obvious, but there is a point to be made. If we are not careful, we will want others to fill the empty space and time that now exists. We want them to be available 24/7/365. We want them to be always calling and chatting with us, to fill the empty spaces that used to be filled by the one who has died. The well becomes a wanting well and not a resource.

If this happens, then we stop caring for the well. We begin to lose the wonder and beauty of it, and it becomes a constant reminder of our loss. This wonderful thing that we created when we became one and committed our lives to creating and building becomes a source of pain and not joy. It becomes a reminder of our loss and not of our blessing.

And then starts the wishing. We wish for one of two things. We wish it would go away and that we would not have to deal with all that it reminds us of. So many try to do this. They run away, wishing they could forget and move on (a topic in another chapter). This is more common if there were problems, struggles, stress, and unresolved issues. This wishing then is worse since we cannot find forgiveness for what we caused and are unable to forgive our spouse for what may have happened.

The other is that we wish for it all to be like it was before. This may result in a person reliving key events, creating shrines through photos and memorabilia. They may try to freeze themselves in a time when all was as perfect as possible. They want the well to be a wishing well, something that will somehow give them back what was lost, by recreating special moments, reliving special events, and so on. This is so dangerous at so many levels. It sometimes means that when the family gathers everything has to be just like it was before the person's death. This is using the well for wishing, using its resources to protect the past and not move into the future.

The well was never meant for this. It was always about providing what was needed to live in this moment, with the purpose of providing the strength to move into the future. It was meant to provide the resources to deal with the struggles so that we could grow and learn as we faced the issues together. It was never about freezing us in time and creating a permanent bubble in time.

Wishing for what is gone is natural. The issue becomes how we handle this. I wish to see my wife. I wish to hear her voice. I wish to taste her cooking again. The list goes on and on. An especially powerful wish is to feel her touch again – a hug, a kiss, a caress, or simply the nearness of her body. This will not happen, and if we are not attentive to this, we can become trapped in the wishing well.

This type of wishing will result in us trying to keep the well intact and functional like it was. To do so, we may begin the tedious process of descending to the bottom, cleaning things, filling the bucket, and then ascending so we can lift the bucket. This becomes emotionally deadly. Remember, you began this well when you were young and healthy, and you knew there were two of you and your love made it possible.

Well-digging is like building a relationship. It is focused on providing resources for life and growth. Grief is about what we lost, but grief is also about learning to use what we still have. We dug the well, and if understood and cared for properly it will bring more joy, peace, and strength. Grief handled properly, will allow us to benefit from the well of our relationship. In fact, grief, used correctly, opens the way to learn how to grow as a result of all that has been done. It is a living well.

I am learning that my grief brings to mind all of these blessings. How I handle the grief will either turn the well into a wanting wishing well and bring harm and greater sadness or it will continue to provide life, hope, and strength for what lies ahead. It is amazing how in one moment grief can cloud one's vision, and the next, create clarity in my vision that both astounds me and brings me joy as I see again the incredible riches that my marriage provides me even now – a well that supplies critical resources to continue living and yes to continue growing.

Tributes

# Obituary

*Written by kids; presented by John P. Hubbard*

Hubbard, Nancy Rae (Smeby) 60, of Grygla, Minnesota, passed away April 11, 2018, after an extended battle with cancer. Nancy was born in Thief River Falls, MN, on November 29, 1957. She graduated from Grygla High School and continued on to receive her bachelor's and master's degree in International Leadership from Crown College. Nancy was married to Perry Hubbard on December 15, 1979; they were married 38 years. Nancy served Global Partners as a missionary for 31 years. She enjoyed spending time with her family and grandchildren. Nancy was actively involved in her ministries and passionately served children in need, helping to found the Ruimveldt Children's Home and Care Center for children infected/affected by HIV/AIDS in 2006. She was a key instructor and developer of the cross-cultural training program for the JIBACAM missions board of the Wesleyan Churches of Latin America. She was known by many around the world and loved by all that knew her. Nancy is survived by her husband, Perry; children, John (Valerie), Jeffrey (Heather), and Jessica; grandchildren, Donovan and Tobias; mother, Doris; three brothers, Jim (Eileen), Lowell (Rochelle), and Paul (Marie); two sisters, Pam (Tim) and JoAnn (John), and other family. Nancy is preceded in death by her father, John Smeby. The family of Nancy wishes to thank all who have offered their support and prayers over the years and the days to come.

# Jeffrey P. Hubbard

*Jer. 29:11*
"For I know the plans I have for you, declared the Lord,
plans to prosper you and not to harm you, plans to give
you hope and a future."

Words have been hard to find to explain the loss of our dear Mother. It brings us a deepening sorrow to know that she is no longer with us, and there has been a great amount of time spent on reflecting and celebrating that she is now pain-free and resting in eternity with our Lord and Savior.

Nancy was a wonderful woman that meant so much to so many people. It wouldn't take long for anyone to go from stranger, to friend, to family. She would quickly become a sister, aunt, mother, or grandmother to those around. She had a deepening understanding of the family of Christ. It is safe to say that only after a brief moment she could leave a lasting impression on whoever she met.

On the surface, our mom had a warm feeling about her that would draw you into her. She had an infectious love and grace that would fill the room and a smile that would melt your heart. She was kind and gentle and cared for everyone around her. Below the surface, she was so much more. She was brave and adventurous as she followed my father to all corners of the world to spread the word of Christ. She was strong as she did this even while fighting cancer. She was selfless as even during her weakest moments she would still ask about others' daily struggles. No matter what the struggle was though, she could always find the good in it. She knew how to give you hope, reassurance, and peace during those times. She knew how to find the light in the darkest times. And she was compassionate as she was always drawn to children, especially those in need. Her faith drove her daily to being such an amazing woman, and she made it look graceful.

Our mom used to tell us how proud she was or me, my brother, and my sister. But what she didn't know was how proud of her we all were. What I am most proud of is not anything that she did, but how she did it. She made everyone around her family; she did it in the service of Christ and she did it with Love.

And now, I am proud to have so many brothers, sisters, aunts, uncles, mothers, and grandmothers to help carry on the legacy of our mother, Nancy.

# Jessica P. Hubbard

My Mother . . .
Even before I put pen to paper
I am overwhelmed with knowing
That the only words I have, are not words enough
That to describe my mother in her full beauty
Would exhaust the English language.
Proud of her heritage, but humble to the core
My mother spoke with calmness,
But walked with strength through the storm
She was a flame, setting others afire
With her ever-burning smile and infectious laughter.
She danced through life with elegance and grace
Pausing only to draw others into her journey
Showing boundless love and selfless courage
She loved loudly, prayed deeply, and trusted completely.
Leaving behind the familiar, she led her life with faith,
Listening to her Father's calling, never doubting His doing
And even when her body was failing,
She found inner strength and peace,
Giving. Inspiring. Never complaining.
As the only daughter, we shared a bond
Tied together by our heartstrings, beating as one
She nurtured me, ever holding my hand
As I cried over broken bones, broken hearts, and broken hopes.
In the midst of those pains, she would guide me
Helping me find healing, comfort, and renewed hope.
In an ever-changing world, she was my security
And I clung to her like a child hugs her blanket.
She eased my worries, listening, laughing, and praying
Knowing just when to say, "Breath, Jessica, Breath."
And although I am not a child,
I am her little girl
Always looking up, longing to be,
Just like my hero.
The void within is indescribable.
As I try to fill it with her memories,

Straining to still hear her voice.
And I find her.
Embedded in the core of who I am.
And who I will be.
She will live on in every moment and milestone to come
Her lessons will guide me,
And her promises will comfort me.
As my heart cries out for her,
As I long to run from this new reality,
I am grateful. I am breathing.
For I was blessed – we were blessed – to have her, as our mother.

# Perry J. Hubbard

*Balance and counterbalance (a tribute to my wife, Nancy).*

"And God saw that man was alone and so he created a helpmate."

We often read these words and we use them as part of sermons on marriage and in marriage ceremonies in the church.

The second part is that a man and a woman will be joined, and they shall be one flesh.

We hear these words as well but until you meet that person, they are phrases that are hard to explain.

It was the same for me until the day I saw Nancy. That day I found someone to help me live. Someone who would help me become the person God knew I could be. Someone to provide the strength to accomplish what one person could not contemplate doing alone.

Nancy brought those phrases to life and filled them with all that God intended them to be. And then I discovered two more words that would define our life together: balance and counterbalance.

Balance is the ability to stand and remain standing no matter what is happening around us. Nancy brought the balance I needed not just to see the vision God had for us but also to be able to follow the vision and not stumble. I also believe that I made this same thing possible for her. Each of us had the need for someone to bring balance to our lives and give us the strength to follow the path God had laid before us.

Nancy made it possible to walk without fear of falling and stumbling. She was always there, even when life became uncertain. Her smile and her confidence in my abilities, my call from God brought stability and focus. She wrote in her application to Global Partners that even though God had not yet called her to missions; she knew that I had been called, and that was enough for her to say she would go wherever God led us, an attitude that guided her life and that God would honor.

This allowed us not only to make the transition from Sierra Leone to Papua New Guinea to Guyana but also to learn three languages and raise three children in very different parts of the world. She brought balance to our family so that we could live wherever God sent us. It also allowed us to move yet again to Panama and serve in Iberoamerica. A balance that created space for all to enter our world and become a part of what God was doing in our lives.

Counterbalance is the ability to allow something or someone to reach farther than possible unaided. To reach what is unreachable without the assistance of something to anchor or hold us when we extend our reach beyond what is possible.

This word clearly defines our life together. We each provided the anchor or counterbalance that allowed us to do more than was possible alone. I know this because I am always reaching farther, trying to do more, wanting to see over the horizon, to climb a little higher. With her in my life, I could take the risks involved because she was the counterbalance, the anchor that was always there.

This action also allowed her to do so much more as well. I watched as she used that knowledge and experience to become a mentor to the wives of students in Sierra Leone and Papua New Guinea – to use that experience to develop a children's choir in one country and puppet ministry in another; to believe in the possibility of starting a children's home for children with HIV, and then draw me into making that a reality.

The truth is that a true counterbalance is so much more than simply a static weight anchored to one spot. A true counterbalance is living and growing. The more I stretched, the stronger she became. She grew and extended her reach to allow me to reach even farther. Nancy's ability to draw people into our lives gave her an unlimited ability to be the anchor I needed to carry out the work God had given us.

This reality of helpmate, unity, balance, and counterbalance has found no better example than in my wife, Nancy. She provided all of this to our family and me. And she has done the same for so many others. She has brought balance to so many people and she has provided the anchor so that they could reach beyond themselves to follow God's leading.

Her favorite verse in these last years was Jeremiah 29:11–13:

> [11]For I know the plans I have for you, declares the Lord, plans to prosper you and not to harm you, plans to give you hope and a future. [12]Then you will call upon me and come and pray to me, and I will listen to you.
> [13]You will seek me and find me when you seek me with all your heart.

This was the focus of her life. To prosper in her relationship with God and make it possible for others to know God and help them know the true meaning of the word prosper, to have a hope and future in God. She is no longer with us, but her legacy is. We have her example of helping others come to God, knowing they will be heard by Him and will find hope and a future.

And while I mourn her passing, she has left me one more great and wonderful blessing; All of you who will continue to bring balance to my life and that of our children, and will allow us, all of us to believe we can reach beyond ourselves and accomplish great things in the kingdom of God.

Dr. Perry J. Hubbard, DMIN Trinity Evangelical Divinity School, Deerfield, Illinois. He and his wife, Nancy, have served as missionaries for over thirty years with Global Partners until her death in 2018. He continues to serve as a missionary in Iberoamerica with a focus on developing missional leaders. He has written fifty books on missions and other topics. For four years he served as the Director of Jibacam, the department of missions of the Wesleyan Churches of Iberoamerica (2015–2019) of which he has been a member since 2001. He also has served as the Principal of the Gbendembu Wesleyan Bible Institute in Sierra Leone (1986–94), and of the Wesleyan Bible College of Papua New Guinea (1995–1999).

"A cut through the platitudes, tell it like it is, journey through grief, fairness, anger, and loss from Dr. Perry Hubbard, as he recounts his personal journey following the loss of his wife, Nancy. "

**Rev. Rod Zottarelli,** MA,
Wellness Coach – Global Partners

"Thoughtful and candid, Perry shares his journey through grief from a man's perspective. With each chapter there is a growing desire to know and to identify with him in his grief."

**Tim Mills,** Psy.D., Clinical Psychologist,
Private Practice, New Direction Counseling, Holland, MI

Made in the USA
Monee, IL
26 August 2020